Rune-Net

TʰE
RUNE PRIMER

A Down-to-Earth Guide to the Runes

by

Sweyn Plowright

Organiser, Rune-Net

Second Edition

© 2006

Rune-Net

ISBN 978-1-84728-246-0

Contents

Acknowledgements

This new edition of the beginners guide was made possible by the suggestions and requests of the members of Rune-Net. Special thanks to my wife Kara, who's unfailing support and understanding have enabled the completion of this and many other projects.

New in this Edition

In the Resources section there are new translations of the Rune Poems, and discussion of some of the authors of esoteric runology. Also, a new chapter with discussion of the many popular myths about the runes.

1   Introduction

Rune-Net is an international online community of students of the Runes. We range in experience from over 25 years study to those who have only just discovered runes. I have taken on the task of writing a basic introduction to the Runes after many requests from new RN members for such a book.

The problem with the many New-Age rune manuals is a general lack of proper research. It does not take a great deal of research to write a reasonable introduction to the runes, yet most have chosen to write superficially about runes while padding out their books with large amounts of New-Age, Wiccan, or Eastern esotericism. They cash in on the popularity of runes, with little regard to their proper cultural and religious context. Those of the modern Northern Traditions see this as not only poor research, but the greatest disrespect for an ancient cultural heritage.

On the other hand, the problem with the more reliable and academic works is that they are often rather dry and obscure for beginners. They tend to throw the beginner in at the deep end. In some ways the more academic popular writers require more caution in reading, as their own agendas and inventions are harder for the beginner to see.

One thing students asked for was a more concise and plain writing style. Most of the books they reviewed were found to be too padded out and wordy. They lacked focus and structure, and made it difficult for students to gain a clear basic picture.

The purpose of this book is to keep it brief and to the point, to stick to the known facts and established conventions, and to avoid unnecessary elaborations, while still including some useful extra information. It should therefore be a concise and handy primer on the runes, with respect for their cultural and religious context. It is intended as a starting point. Not a complete volume of everything, but a basic foundation from which anyone can begin their studies from an informed perspective. With this grounding, the student should be able to read further, with the discretion to sort some of the wheat from the chaff.

2   Importance of Context

The Runes were used by the Germanic tribes from at least 1800 years ago until about 1000 years ago, when they were increasingly replaced by the Roman alphabet we use today. Their use survived in various forms in parts of Scandinavia until the 1700s. The Germanic tribes inhabited a large area of Northern Europe and were distinguished by their culture and language. The descendants of the Germanic tribes became the peoples of the countries whose native languages are Germanic. The main modern Germanic languages are English, German, Dutch, Danish, Swedish, Norwegian, and Icelandic.

The Runes were seen by the Germanic peoples as more than a system of writing. They were an integral part of their magical and religious culture. Although not much is actually known about their practices, enough examples have survived to give us an idea about the importance and respect the Runes held. We know that they were often used in magic, spells of protection, and for success in battle, as well as for healing.

The word "rune" can also mean a mystery or secret. Not only are there written characters we call runes, but spells and incantations are sometimes called runes. The Futhark runes were a special kind of mystery.

While studying rune manuals, we must be wary of those claiming to teach "traditional" runic practices, as we must ask about their sources. Many New-Age manuals will invent or borrow ideas, and claim them to be ancient tradition, either without mentioning sources, or by a wild interpretation of an obscure part of an ancient source. Always check these sources and decide if they actually support the writer's assertions.

There are also those who are genuinely involved in creating or re-creating traditions based on our limited knowledge of the Heathen Germanic culture. These folk are actively reviving the ancient religion while acknowledging that they cannot re-create the complete picture. They use as much original source literature as possible to reconstruct what they can, and fill in the gaps with sensitivity to the original, while keeping it practical for the modern person. These groups are loosely termed "Asatru", meaning true to the Aesir (Germanic Gods).

Mythologically, the origin of the Runes is described in the Havamal, part of a collection of Icelandic Viking mythology called the poetic Edda. Odin, senior god of the Aesir, tells of his ordeal leading to his gaining the Runes:

I know that I hung, upon the windswept tree

Nights all of nine, by my spear pierced

And given to Odin, myself unto my Self

On that tree of which none know

whence its roots do run

With bread none saved me, nor with drinking horn

I looked into the depths

I took up the Runes

Screaming I took them

I fell back therefrom

Although the Eddas are late Germanic, specifically Viking, they are the most complete view of the Northern Heathen world left to us. For this reason, the Eddas are the major source literature for most Asatru groups. It is vital to become familiar with the Eddas as a first step in coming to understand the context of the runic world. Without this most basic foundation, the study of the Runes will be not just superficial, but somewhat pointless. To dabble in the Runes without a good knowledge of their cultural and religious background is disrespectful to the ancestors, their gods, and the Asatruar who are striving to live in harmony with those ancestors and gods.

Any magico-religious system must have a cultural home, one that can claim a right of respect. The eclectic New-Agers will argue that they have a right to incorporate any system, or parts of systems, into their own practice. Maybe so, but do they have a right to pass their half understood version of those systems on to others, and claim to speak with authority? Some of the Native American tribes have stated that the New-Age piracy of their traditions amounts to an act of war. When practices with a deep cultural significance are taken out of their cultural context and popularised, it threatens the survival and understanding of those practices in their original setting, and dilutes their deeper meaning.

As Asatru, in its widest sense, is the only tradition seeking to understand the cultural contexts which were native to the Runes, it is only reasonable to acknowledge Asatru should have a right to the guardianship of their future development. This means that if we want the Runes to survive as a meaningful system, we need to experience them with some understanding of Asatru. We do not all necessarily need to adopt Asatru as our own religion, but we do need at least to be able to function within it.

There is another reason to take the trouble to learn. The old sources give us the clear impression that runes are not to be messed with lightly. Odin is the deity of war, and of dark magic. He is tricky and subtle. The Runes are spoken of as dangerous and likely to harm the unprepared.

It should be kept in mind that, like other areas of Asatru, the runic practices of today have been developed from very limited original sources. While these sources can give us many insights if viewed with a knowledge of Germanic culture and religion, it remains a fact that current esoteric runology is a product of the speculations of a few writers on the meanings of the rune poems, rune names, and a few obscure references in other literature.

The surviving examples of runic inscriptions may provide tantalising and useful hints, but these are by no means clear proof of occult practices. In fact some of the foremost academic authorities do not believe that there was a significant runic magical system. This is an extreme position, however. On the balance of evidence, it does seem clear that the runes did always carry magical connotations, and were part of the magico-religious culture for centuries, being maintained as a common tradition.

On the other extreme, the idea of an ancient rune-magician cult or organisation is extremely far fetched, as are claims of the ancient traditions surviving in secret. Such myths were popular in the early 1900s among many occult groups, who claimed their knowledge and authority as coming from secret chiefs in the Himalayas, or ancient secret documents rediscovered, or ancient knowledge surviving as family tradition. Such fables have been used so often to support claims of authority, or privileged knowledge, that they invariably do nothing but harm the credibility of esoteric research.

Somewhere between the extremes is a position where we can find reasonably solid ground on which to build. This position can be found by looking at the sources, and casting a critical eye over the way these have been interpreted by the more relevant writers. In this way we can see what remains of the ancient tradition, and help to build upon modern convention in order to harmonise our use of the Runes with both the old Germanic culture and modern Asatru.

As we look at the modern writers, we need to identify their sources and influences. This may sometimes seem to be harsh or even negative. This is not the intention. Sometimes we need to clear the ground before laying foundations. All of the popular writers on esoteric runology have introduced significant non-Germanic or personal inventions and influences. This is not necessarily bad in itself, but we should have the choice to accept or reject those imports on the basis of their origins and relationship to the system as a whole. We should not just accept anything as "authentic" on the word of any self-proclaimed authority.

3   Old Sources

Read the Havamal at least, and buy the Poetic Edda. The best value translations of the Poetic Edda are by Hollander from Texas Uni Press, or by Larrington of Oxford Uni Press. The Eddas contain most of the mythological context surrounding the Runes including the Havamal. It will also give a feel for the culture of the time at the end of the runic period.

Read Tacitus "The Germania" to get a feel for the Germanic culture in the early runic period, first century C.E. (C.E = common era, B.C.E. = before common era; - an academic non-Christian alternative to AD and BC).

For an excellent academic introduction to runes, RI Page "Runes" is the best value. Professor Page has put together a lot of interesting and accurate historical information in a very readable and affordable little book.

These books are really a bare minimum for anyone considering starting rune studies. They are easy to find or order from a bookstore, and fairly inexpensive. Look up the details in the Resources section toward the end of this book.

The rune rows themselves show us the shapes, order, and Aetts (groups). The first and most popular row is the Elder Futhark, which was used from about 2000 years ago until about the 8th century. After a few centuries of relative stability, the runes diverged from the original, resulting in the 16 rune Younger Futhark in the Viking lands, and the 33 rune Anglo-Saxon Futhorc in England and Frisia.

The preferred row for modern esoteric study is the Elder Futhark. The rune row is called a futhark as its first six runes spell F, U, Th, A, R, K.

The most important sources for the interpretation of the Runes are the rune poems. Unfortunately, no poem exists for the Elder Futhark. We have to rely on the poems of the later rows, and reconstruct the likely names and meanings for the Elder row.

3.1 Elder Futhark

The Elder Futhark is usually presented in three groups of eight (Aetts = families).

First Aett

f u th a r k g w

Second Aett

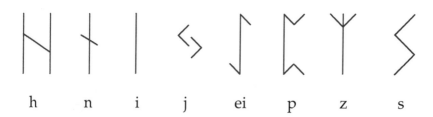

h n i j ei p z s

Third Aett

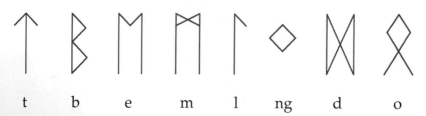

t b e m l ng d o

The few surviving inscriptions, and the reconstruction of the early Germanic language confirm the sounds of these runes.

The vowels (short, long) are roughly; **u** = (book, tool), **a** = (father, art), **i** = (hit, heat), **ei** = (*not certain,* probably between **e** and **i**), **e** = (ed, air), **o** = (hot, caught). Use English or German pronunciation, not the American (hot = haht).

The consonants are as for English except **j** is pronounced like the **y** in "year", and the German **j** (ja = yes). Also **z** which is thought to be somewhere between English r and z, and became the final **R** in Early Norse. This explains the movement in the Younger row of the **Elk** to the end, and its renaming to **Yew.**

Nothing is known about the original esoteric names or meanings, but there is enough information in the later rows to reconstruct the most likely names and meanings. The names can then be rendered in the reconstructed early Germanic language. The reconstruction has become the most commonly used convention for modern esoteric runologists.

3.2 *Younger Futhark*

In Scandinavia during the 700s, the Vikings developed a
shorter version of the Futhark with 16 runes.

First Aett

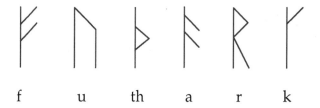

f   u   th   a   r   k

Second Aett

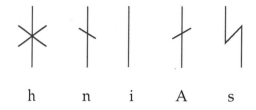

h   n   i   A   s

Third Aett

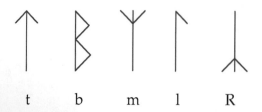

t   b   m   l   R

Some of the staves have been altered from the Elder row. They were, however, careful to preserve some features of the 3 Aett system, particularly the initial runes of each Aett. The Aetts are sometimes referred to as Frey's Aett, Hagall's Aett, and Tyr's Aett.

The Younger Futhark also came with names and poems for each rune, in Old Norwegian and Old Icelandic. By comparing the various rune names and poems, we can make an educated guess at the likely names and meanings of the Elder Futhark runes.

This common Younger row was also developed into a row of simplified forms for practical writing in Sweden and Norway.

3.3 Anglo-Saxon Futhorc

By about 600 - 700 CE, the Anglo-Saxons and Frisians were developing their own version of the Runes.

First Aett

| f | u | th | o | r | c | g | w |

Second Aett

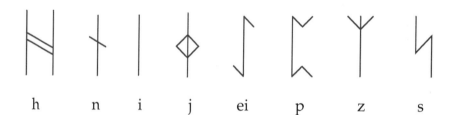

| h | n | i | j | ei | p | z | s |

Third Aett

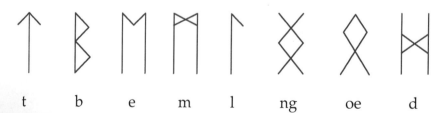

| t | b | e | m | l | ng | oe | d |

Extra Runes

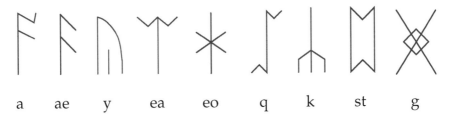

| a | ae | y | ea | eo | q | k | st | g |

The Anglo-Saxon Futhorc has up to 9 extra runes added, making 33. The first 24 are almost identical to the Elder Futhark. The vowel changes which occurred in Anglo-Saxon created a need for extra characters.

This Futhorc also comes with names and rune poems. The Anglo-Saxon rune poems are the most revealing sources for the esoteric interpretation of the Runes.

Like all of the runic traditions, there were many variations in the forms of many of the runes. These should be looked into in some of the more academic text books. It should be realised that there were no strict standards as there are for modern alphabets. The variation indicates that there was no central authority or cult maintaining the system. Despite this, there was quite a lot of consistency, pointing toward a valued and well-kept tradition.

3.4 Rune Names

We have no record of the names of the Elder Futhark runes. We cannot really be certain they had any. We do, however, have names for the Younger and Anglo-Saxon runes, & the Gothic alphabet. The consistency between these systems leads us to believe that they reflect and preserve much of the tradition of the Elder row.

Neither can we be certain of the language spoken at the time of the Elder runes. Very few inscriptions survive, and these tend to be too short to reveal much detail about the language. We do know that the common tongue was made up of mutually intelligible dialects across the Germanic tribes. Linguists have reconstructed this "proto-Germanic" language by comparing the various later Germanic languages and applying the principles of linguistic change over time.

Thus, by looking at the Anglo-Saxon (Old English) and Younger (Old Norse) rune rows and comparing their names and meanings, we can make an educated guess at the most likely Elder Futhark names. Then with a knowledge of the reconstructed proto-Germanic, we can get a fair estimate of the form those names took.

Rune Names:

English	Meaning	Norse	Meaning
Feoh	cattle/money	Fe	cattle/money
Ur	ox	Ur	drizzle/slag
Thorn	thorn	Thurs	giant
Os	god/mouth	Ass	god
Rad	ride	Reidh	ride
Cen	torch	Kaun	sore
Gyfu	gift		
Wynn	joy		
Haegl	hail	Hagall	hail
Nyd	need	Naudhr	need
Is	ice	Iss	ice
Ger	year	Ar	year
Eoh	yew		
Peordh	? game/tune		
Eolhx	elk sedge		
Sigel	sun	Sol	sun
Tir	a god	Tyr	a god
Beorc	birch	Bjarkan	birch
Eh	horse		
Monn	man	Madhr	man
Lagu	sea	Logr	sea
Ing	Ing(god)		
Daeg	day		
Ethel	inheritance		
		Yr	Yew

As we can see, the names and order agree quite well. We can now reconstruct the Elder names:

*fehu	cattle/money
*uruz	wild ox
*þurisaz	giant
*ansuz	god
*raido	riding
? *kenaz/*kaunaz	? torch/sore
*gebo	gift
*wunjo	joy
*hagalaz	hail
*nauðiz	need, necessity
*isa-	ice
*jera	year/harvest
*eihwaz	yew tree
? *perþ-	? unknown
? *algiz/ *elhaz	? swan/elk
*sowilo	sun
*tiwaz	the god Tiw/Tyr
*berkan-	birch
*ehwaz	horse
*mannaz	man
*laguz	water
*ingwaz	the god Ing
*dagaz	day
*oþala	inheritance

Variations on this reconstruction can be found in several of the books in the bibliography. Most of the academic authors are in close agreement with it. It is important to realise that the reconstruction is based on educated guesswork. Nobody can know for sure, as the original names were never recorded.

Note 1: þ = thorn, the sound of **th** as in "thorn".

Note 2: ð = eth, the sound of **th** as in "then". Often also written as **dh.**

Note 3: It is convention to show a word is reconstructed by putting an asterisk in front. Eg, *fehu.

Note 4: The final two runes are sometimes swapped in their order with Dagaz last. There is no way to say which is more "correct", but most of the oldest inscriptions have Othala last, and most modern writers prefer this order.

3.5 Rune Poems

Although they may have started as an aid to memorising the names, the rune poems are the major source of information about the possible esoteric meaning of the Runes. It is likely that the Runes were used for divination and magic from the earliest times.

I have provided the following new translations specifically for this book. The original texts with translator's notes are included in the Resources section later in this book.

The three rune poems are fairly different in character. The Old English one expands on the moral nature of the rune name. The Old Icelandic one uses "kennings" or riddles, three for each rune. The Old Norwegian uses a kenning followed by a phrase chosen more for the rhyme than the meaning.

Kennings can be open to interpretation, or even have multiple meanings. For instance, Fé is "flood-tide's sign". Fé means wealth, which in the earliest times meant cattle. Some may think of cattle floating down a river as the sign of a flood. I think of Vikings attacking up a river, carried on the rising flood-tide, to gain wealth, then making a quick getaway on the ebb-tide.

The rune poems in the next pages are listed in the following order:

Elder Futhark Rune shape
Reconstructed Elder name

Old English Rune Poem (OERP) Anglo-Saxon Futhorc
Old Icelandic Rune Poem (OIRP) Younger Futhark
Old Norwegian Rune Poem (ONRP) Younger Futhark

*fehu = wealth, cattle, money

Feoh: **Money** is a comfort to humans all;
but each one should deal it out abundantly,
if he wants before the Lord to chance judgement. OERP

Fe: **Money** is kinsmens' quarrel/ and flood-tide's token/
and necromancy's road. OIRP

Fe: **Money** causes kinsmen's quarrel; the wolf is reared in
the forest. ONRP

ᚢ

*uruz = aurochs, wild ox

ᚢ Ur: **Aurochs** is single-minded and over-horned,
a very dangerous animal - fights with horns -
a notorious moor-treader; that is an intrepid being! OERP

ᚢ Ur: **drizzle** is the clouds' tears/ and the harvest's ruin/ and
the herder's hate. OIRP

ᚢ Ur: **slag** is from bad iron; oft lopes the reindeer over frozen
snow. ONRP

þ

*þurisaz = a giant

þ Thorn: **Thorn** is extremely sharp, for any warrior
to grab it, evil; excessively fierce
to any man who amongst them rests. OERP

þ Thurs: **giant** is womens' illness/ and a cliff-dweller/ and
Vardhrun's husband. OIRP

þ Thurs: **giants** cause women's sickness; few are made
cheerful by adversity. ONRP

*ansuz = a god

Os: **Deity/Mouth** is the origin of every language,
Wisdom's support and counsellors' consolation
and to any warrior gladness and confidence. OERP

Ass: **god** (Ódhinn) is progenitor/ and Ásgardh's chief/ and
Valhall's leader. OIRP

Oss: **estuary** is the way for most on journeys; and the
scabbard is the sword's. ONRP

ᚱ

*raido = riding

ᚱ Rad: **Riding** is, in the hall, for every man
easy, and very hard for him who sits upon
a powerful horse over miles of road. OERP

ᚱ Reidh: **riding** is sitting joyful/ and a speedy trip/ and the
horse's toil. OIRP

ᚱ Reidh: **riding** they say is for horses worst; Reginn
hammered out the best sword. ONRP

⟨

*kenaz/*kaunaz = torch/sore

ᚻ Cen: **Lamp** is to the living all, known by its flame,
pale and bright; it burns most often
where the noble folk within relax. OERP

ᚲ Kaun: **sore** is childrens' illness/ and a battle journey/ and
putrescence's house.OIRP

ᚲ Kaun: **sore** is the disfiguring of children; adversity renders
a person pale. ONRP

*gebo = gift

X Gyfu: **Gift** for men is adornment and complement,
support and dignity; and for all the dispossessed
forgiveness and sustenance, who would otherwise have
nothing. OERP

*wunjo = joy

P Wynn: **Joy** is had by one who knows few troubles,
sores or sorrow, and has for himself
reputation and happiness, and also a fine secure home. OERP

*hagalaz = hail

Haegl: **Hail** is the whitest of seeds;
it spins out of heaven's air, rolling with the wind's blows;
it is turned into water thereafter. OERP

Hagall: **hail** is cold seed/ and a sleet shower/ and snake's
illness. OIRP

Hagall: **hail** is the coldest of seeds; Christ shaped the
world (the heavens) in fore times. ONRP

†

*nauðiz = need, necessity

† Nyd: **Need** is tight in the breast;
but it often happens for humans' children
to help and to save each, if they listen to it early. OERP

† Naudh: **need** is a bondswoman's yearning/ and a difficult circumstance/ and drudging work. OIRP

† Naudh: **need** renders little choice; the naked will freeze in the frost. ONRP

|

*isa- = ice

| Is: **Ice** is over-cold, extremely slippery;
it glistens glass-clear, most like gems;
it is a floor wrought by frost, fair to look upon. OERP

| Iss: **ice** is a river's bark/ and a wave's thatch/ and doomed
men's downfall. OIRP

| Iss: **ice** is called a bridge broad; the blind need to be led.
ONRP

*jera = year or harvest

† Ger: **Year/Harvest** is men's hope, when God,
holy heaven's king, lets the earth give
shining fruit to the warriors and the poor. OERP

† Ar: **harvest** is men's bounty/ and a good summer/ and a
full-grown field. OIRP

† Ar: **harvest** is men's bounty; I guess that generous was
Fródhi. ONRP

*eihwaz = yew tree

Eoh: **Yew** is on the outside an unsmooth tree,
hard in the earth holding fast, fire's keeper,
by roots buttressed, a joy on the estate. OERP

Yr: **yew** is a bent bow/ and fragile iron/ and arrow's
Farbauti. OIRP

Yr: **yew** is the winter-greenest wood; and is found
wanting, when it burns, to ignite. ONRP

*perþ- = possibly a board game, or a tune

Peorth: **Peorth** is ever play and laughter
to the proud (missing), where warriors sit
in the beer-hall merrily together. OERP

*algiz/ *elhaz = possibly elk

Eolhx: **Elk**-sedge is native most often in the fen,
it grows in water; it wounds grimly,
burning with blood any warrior
who, in any way, grabs at it. OERP

ᛋ

*sowilo = Sun

ᛋ Sigel: **Sun/sail** for seamen is ever cause for hope,
when they ferry it over the fishes' bath,
until the sea-stallion brings them to land. OERP

ᛋ Sol: **sun** is the clouds' shield / and a shining ray/ and ice's
old enemy. OIRP

ᛋ Sol: the **sun** is the land's light; I bow to holy judgement.
ONRP

*tiwaz = the god Tiw

↑ **Tir** is a particular token; it holds trust well
with noble folk; it is ever on a journey
over nights' mists; it never deceives. OERP

↑ **Tyr** is a one-handed god/ and wolf's leftovers/ and the
temple's chief. OIRP

↑ **Tyr** is a one-handed god; oft will a smith be blowing.
ONRP

*berkan- = birch tree

ᛒ Beorc: **Birch** is lacking fruit; it bears even so
sprouts without seed; its boughs beautiful,
high on top, fairly decorated;
grown with leaves, close to the sky. OERP

ᛒ Bjarkan: **birch** is a leaf covered limb/ and a slender tree/
and a spritely wood. OIRP

ᛒ Bjarkan: **birch** is leaf-greenest of limbs; Loki bore
treachery's fortune. ONRP

ᛗ

*ehwaz = horse

ᛗ Eh: **Horse** is, before warriors, the joy of noble folk,
a horse hoof-proud, when the warriors around it,
wealthy on steeds, exchange speech;
and it is, to the wanderer, ever a benefit. OERP

*mannaz = man, human being

Monn: **Man** is, in his mirth, to his kinfolk dear;
yet shall each disappoint the other,
accordingly the Lord wills, by his law,
that the poor flesh be entrusted to the earth. OERP

Madhr: **man** is man's pleasure/ and mould's increase/ and a ship's embellisher. OIRP

Madhr: **man** is mould's increase; great is the grip of the hawk. ONRP

ᛚ

*laguz = sea

ᛚ Lagu: **Sea** is by folk thought wide indeed,
if they should dare to go in a ship unsteady,
and the waves terribly frighten them,
and the sea-stallion heed not its bridle. OERP

ᛚ Logr: **sea** is a welling water/ and a wide kettle/ and a fish's
field. OIRP

ᛚ Logr: **water** is, when falling out of a mountain, a cascade;
and costly ornaments are of gold. ONRP

*ingwaz = the god Ing (Frey)

Ing: **Ing** was first with the East-Danes
seen they say, until he later east
over the sea departed; wagon followed after;
thus warriors named that hero. OERP

*dagaz = day

Daeg: **Day** is the Lord's herald, dear to men,
the great Judge's light, merriment and hope
to the fortunate and the poor, enjoyed by all. OERP

*oþala = inheritance, estate, ancestral land

 Ethel: **Homestead** is over-dear to each man,
if he may there justice and courtesies
enjoy in a mansion in frequent prosperity. OERP

3.6   *Inscriptions*

The problem with inscriptions is that they are often difficult to interpret. There were no spelling conventions, and messages tended to be short. The meanings of some inscriptions have never been agreed upon by the experts. The cynical Prof. Page talks about "imaginative" runologists, who insist on seeing magic whenever they cannot translate an inscription.

Although there is disagreement among academics, Thorsson does put forward some good arguments and examples in favour of a magical interpretation for some inscriptions in "Runelore".

Most surviving inscriptions are simple memorials of the form "XX raised this stone in memory of [relative] YY, [son/daughter] of ZZ, who was [worthy attribute]".

4   The Runic Revival

The modern runic traditions have various origins. Some of these origins are based on the interpretation of academic knowledge. Some are based on less reliable guesswork. In keeping with its purpose as a beginners guide, this chapter will take a brief look at the better known sources. Students should read further from the book list.

4.1   The Armanen

During the general occult revival of the early 1900s, Guido von List was inspired to publish his own vision of the Runes as part of a spiritual revitalisation of the German-speaking people.

Influenced by the works of Wagner and Nietsche, von List's system fitted in well with the pan-German nationalistic romanticism which was to evolve into Nazism by the 1930s. These runes became potent symbols of organisations within the Third Reich, and led to runes becoming a taboo subject for many years after the war.

List's system was based on the Younger Futhark, with some odd variant rune forms, and the addition of two runes to make 18.

His interpretations were largely based on the 18 riddles or spells mentioned in the Havamal. These are called "lays" (ljoð) in the original, and were unlikely to have referred to futhark runes. The word "rune" can also refer to a spell or mystery.

This method of interpretation, and the influence of Indian philosophy, popular in occult circles at the time, make the system now seem rather quaint and no more "authentic" than modern New-Age fusions.

Like the Theosophists and other occult groups of the period, the Armanen system adapted techniques from Yoga, and incorporated them into their practices.

4.2 The Current Revival

The current runic revival really began with the explosion of interest in the 1970s in JRR Tolkien's novels. The growing New-Age movement was ripe for powerful magical fantasy. Runes featured prominently in these books. This was not surprising; Tolkien was a professor of Nordic literature and drew heavily on Germanic mythological themes.

The popularisation of rune magic began in the early 1980s. There had been the occasional rune manual before that, but these had been largely focused on the Armanic system.

Around 1980, Michael Howard's early books were the first popular manuals to attempt to look at the Runes from their Germanic historical and mythological perspective. These early works look very rough to us now, with rather unusual shapes, inconsistent order, and not all of the runes discussed. But the 24 Elder runes and 3 Aetts are mentioned. His interpretations are of more interest, as they do seem to influence many of the later writers. His later work (1985) is much better.

In 1982, Ralph Blum produced a commercial hit with a slim book packaged with a bag of rune tiles. His book took the standard Elder Futhark , added a "blank rune" to represent wyrd or fate, and reorganised the row into a 5 by 5 grid. Although he mentions the futhark order and the 3 by 8 traditional arrangement in the introduction, he chooses to completely rearrange them for his system.

His interpretations are superficial, and seem to owe more to I Ching than to the Germanic system. This makes it an easy way for people to get started, and accounts for its huge success. However, to those interested in the revival of the Northern Traditions, he is seen as a cultural pirate, cashing in on our traditions at the expense of their integrity.

A turning point came in 1984 with the publication of Edred Thorsson's book on Rune Magic "Futhark". This was the first popular manual to include really accurate academic information on the Runes. Thorsson holds a PhD in Germanic studies, and his education shows.

His 1987 "Runelore" builds on the wealth of information. Although beginners have found these works somewhat dry, they have become part of modern esoteric runology.

Like other modern occult writers Thorsson is not without critics. His academic material is so good, and he writes with such authority, that it is easy to take the whole lot as "authentic". Reconstructionists point out that much of Thorsson's system is not based on elder sources, but like the New-Age fusions, is a composite of various non-Germanic magical ideas with Jungian psychology and his own inventions.

The ideas of Thorsson most often criticised by Asatruar are; his Cabala-like tree with its connecting paths, his Armanen style rune yoga, and his insistence on tying the Runes to a modern Western Left Hand Path philosophy. Some see his Germanic psychology as a lot like Jung's model with Norse names slotted in.

Reconstructionists feel that Thorsson tends to start his books with excellent historical information, but then he goes on to present a system with little connection to the source tradition, without clearly identifying his speculations, implying that they are somehow "authentic". Hard liners would argue that he has done much the same as the New-Agers in inventing "tradition". The more moderate are grateful for the academic parts, and choose how much of the rest to use in their own practices.

Some of these problems have led to friction with many Asatru groups. Thorsson explains in Runelore that he originally intended to work organically within Asatru, but now finds that he and his followers must work as "outsiders" and carry on the "genuine" tradition alone. Many Asatruar see this as somewhat arrogant. However, "Futhark", and "Runelore" remain the best sources for detailed research once the speculative parts are identified.

Since the mid 1980s, there have been many New-Age rune manuals. Although some have interesting insights, few are worth much comment. They have so far been characterised by a superficial approach, poor research, and a mix and match attitude that removes the Runes from their magico-religious culture. Often these writers will merely take the rune basics from another manual, and slot it into whatever system interests them; tarot, Wicca, shamanism, etc.

While nobody can claim to have a complete authentic runic system, we can at least become familiar with the old sources, and identify the new accretions in order to decide for ourselves which parts to adopt. In this way we can avoid falling into the trap of cultism, or the self-delusion of the fantasy traditions. If we want to defend our heritage from New-Age piracy, we must be equally wary of our own urges to accept attractive inventions without question.

We need not reject the new out of hand, but neither should we count on a neat, complete system packaged for us. The way forward is to work within the Northern culture, and enable the re-emergence of a natural runic tradition from the foundation of the surviving lore.

5   Concepts

The main concepts necessary for an understanding of the esoteric culture of the runes are Orlog, Wyrd, and Hamingja. These are inter-related but separate ideas lying at the heart of the Germanic/Runic way of understanding the interplay of events, life, and the Runes.

5.1   Orlog

Ørlög is the Old Norse word meaning "primal law" or "primal layer". It is the most basic fabric of reality. All things exist and happen according to the known and unknown laws of nature.

5.2   Wyrd

Wyrd is the Old English word describing the hidden connections between events. The word is cognate (a direct linguistic relative) with the German "verden", to become.

Wyrd is often translated as "fate", but there is more to it. Heathens believed that we create our own fate. Although we cannot escape it, we do have the power to shape it.

Northern mythology revolves around the fact that even the gods cannot escape their wyrd. Christians tended to have more of an understanding of a fixed plan of the future, and interpreted wyrd to mean "destiny". Later, the sense of interconnectedness of all things was lost and wyrd became "weird" meaning strange or supernatural.

The three Norns weave the web of wyrd blindly according to Orlog. Shakespeare's "Macbeth" is a clear illustration of the action of wyrd. The three "weird sisters" give Macbeth some information, and he creates his wyrd by acting on it. See the play!

5.3   Hamingja

Hamingja is a Norse word perhaps best translated as "personal power". It is a combination of luck, skill, and success, both earned and inherited.

It is sometimes spoken of as a kind of subtle body, and has even been associated with shape-shifting. For our purposes it is more useful to think of it in its sense of a manifestation of the will of the individual empowered by their wyrd. A strong hamignja also depends on reputation, and like reputation can be built up with a little steady effort. It allows us to achieve our goals, and survive the storms, with seeming effortlessness (like magic).

Understanding the hamingja, you will understand why success breeds success.

6   Esoteric Runes

Using mainly the rune poems, modern rune users have developed interpretations of each rune for the purposes of divination and magic. Here we will look at the basic essence of each.

6.1   Interpretations

ᚠ Fehu. Money.

Although the earliest wealth was measured in cattle, and this word originally had that meaning, the sense used here is simply money.

In magic or divination, Fehu is fairly straightforward. Financial matters, increase in wealth. Money is very useful in working the will, but let us not forget the advice that good fortune should be shared.

ᚢ Uruz. Wild Ox. Aurochs, Slag, Drizzle.

This is much harder to reconstruct from original sources. The three poems are quite different. There is some consensus, however, that the Anglo-Saxon version may be closer to the original.

The wild ox has attributes of courage and determination. This leads to the idea of asserting the will in Midgard (the World), making plans and carrying them out, or pushing ahead in the face of opposition. It is a useful rune for gaining strength.

ᚦ Thurisaz. Thurse, Giant, Thorn.

Another rune with different meanings, but a general agreement that it is not pleasant to tangle with.

Modern writers tend to agree on a meaning of focused power. This can be used to break through obstacles. It is also useful in curses. Like the thurses (giants), the force once unleashed may not be easy to control.

ᚪ Ansuz. A god, Mouth, Odin.

Communication, the divine. Inspiration was considered a form of sacred communication.

Odin is the deity of the runes. He is also a god of poetry, magic, wisdom, and inspiration. This can be used to represent messages on the mundane level, through to matters sacred to the tradition. The Runes themselves, and the study of them, are part of this idea.

ᚱ Raido. Riding, Carriage.

Travel, a vehicle, the need to move in order to progress.

Wagons were often associated with the gods. This rune can represent a physical journey, or a significant but directed change from where we are to where we want to be. It can be useful in matters of transport, your car for instance.

‹ Kenaz? Torch, Sore.

The poems are contradictory, but could be connected by the idea of a burning point.

Most writers seem to follow Howard's lead in taking the Old English poem as the main source. This can be the torch of directed creativity, or the light at the end of the tunnel. It could refer to intellectual knowledge or enlightenment.

✕ Gebo. Gift.

A gift, appreciation, honour, a show of respect or affection.

Our ancestors saw generosity as a great virtue. The meaning of this rune is fairly plain, but there are many kinds of gift. The Havamal says that a gift demands a gift. This should not be a case of "owing" a debt. When given freely, a gift will attract enough rewards. Give without expectation.

ᚹ Wunjo. Pleasure, Joy.

The poem suggests the joy of a comfortable life.

Many of us tend to take things for granted. Our ancestors, like people of many other countries today, were thankful for the basic comforts of life when they had them. This could represent any kind of joy or improvement in life. It can be used to promote fellowship, and an appreciation for what we have.

ᚺ Hagalaz. Hail.

An interesting combination of destructive and creative forces. The second Aett begins here with a change of mood.

Hail is cold and unpleasant; its destructive power has always been obvious to farmers. Yet it is described as a grain, and it brings water, a suggestion of new growth. This is the storm to break the drought, a crisis clearing the air to start a new phase of progress.

† Nauthiz. Need, Necessity.

Like the previous rune, a grim start with a message of hope.

Need is a restriction of choices which force us to make difficult decisions, and act with discipline. If acted on early, the discipline we adopt can itself bring benefits beyond the relief of the immediate condition. Necessity can also be the motivation to achieve change for the better.

| Isa. Ice.

The bleak theme continues with this mixture of beauty and danger.

In a wider mythological context, ice is one of the primal elements (with fire) in the creation of the world. Ice makes for difficult travel, and can represent a halt to progress, or a need to be cautious of a situation that looks attractive, but may harbour hidden risks. It may be a good time to stop and appreciate the view.

Jera. Year, Harvest.

Gain and growth, return on investment.

Hard work, good judgement, and some luck result in a profit to the investor, and the whole community gains. There is also the implication of the completion of a cycle. This obviously does not refer to a quick profit, but a longer-term project.

Eihwaz. Yew tree.

Toughness, stability, resistant to burning, with a deadly sting.

Yew trees can protect a property from fire. Yew bows were the weapon protecting the English soldiers in countless battles. This can be useful when there is a need to stand one's ground. There is also a long association between yews and graveyards, and the rune is given a connection with death by most writers.

Perthro. Board game, musical tune.

Friendly competition, happy social gathering,

We cannot be certain about the meaning of the name, but the image of the poem is clear. Games of chance and skill tested and built the wyrd and ability of warriors. Friendship, and loyalty also increased in the traditional hall. It is important to cultivate friendships, and realise that their wyrd will affect yours.

Algiz, Elhaz. Elk-sedge? Blade grass.

Self defence. Protection.

The poem describes a plant well able to defend itself. Modern writers also tend to note that the shape resembles the Heathen posture of calling to the gods. It could be used to protect yourself or others. It could also be applied to the martial arts. Let an opponent's eagerness to grasp be their downfall.

Sowilo. The Sun.

Victory, good fortune.

In the Germanic traditions, unlike most Southern systems, the Sun is feminine and the Moon masculine. The great light is a sign to lift the spirit, and a symbol of victory. To sailors it is a guide.

Tiwaz. The god Tiw (Tyr) the one-handed.

Battle, justice, self-sacrifice.

Tyr sacrificed his hand by placing it in the mouth of the wolf Fenrir so that the gods could bind it. Steadfast and unswerving, this is the god of a just fight.

ᛒ Berkana, Berkano. Birch.

Beauty, Birth, Beginnings.

Birch is often associated with fertility and goddesses. The rune is now most often used to symbolise birth, creativity, female sexuality, and new beginnings.

ᛗ Ehwaz. Horse.

Co-operation, loyalty, travel for pleasure, pilgrimage.

The horse was sacred to many Germanic tribes. Tacitus mentions their use in divination. The poem connects it with nobility, and as a comfort to the restless. This can mean a spiritual journey, or a close partnership or friendship like horse and rider.

ᛗ Mannaz. Man, Human.

Humanity, culture, higher self.

The strengths and weaknesses that make us human. The human is that which is of most value to us, but which must be lost in the end. This could also refer to the advice "know thyself". This is usually applied to the spiritual quest. Also a reminder that we are still one with the physical world.

ᛚ Laguz. Sea, Lake.

Water, the intuitive.

Water was used to bless a new child (ausa vatni = sprinkle water). The depths of water are mysterious, and often likened to the subconscious mind. There is curiosity of the unknown, and also danger. Some writers also identify this rune as Laukaz = Leek, but the evidence is fairly thin. It is often used for issues of mental health

◇

Ingwaz. Hero, Ingvi Frey.

Nature, peace, plenty.

The poem describes a hero named Ing. We need to look at the mythology to seek further. Ingvi Frey is the god of fertility, peace, and plenty. Frey is described as "veraldar godh" or worldly god, and represents male sexuality. This is especially used in men's issues.

Dagaz. Day.

Daylight, clarity, revelation, safety, hope.

Daylight is comfort to rich and poor. Things seem less threatening, and much becomes clear. This can dispel ignorance, or expose deceit. It implies an increased level of awareness.

Othala. Inheritance, homestead.

The right to enjoy one's inheritance.

Inheritance includes land, family traits, and customs. We should appreciate the many gifts bestowed by our ancestors. This rune enters into matters of tradition and long-term property. It is a stable foundation on which to build.

Summary

These interpretations are only the briefest and most obvious essence. They are derived directly from the rune poems, with some added influence from modern Asatru convention.

Other writers have elaborated by using the Germanic mythology, while some have used other foreign and less fitting sources. It is now your task to study the Germanic sources and look at various writers' runic interpretations to decide how much is harmonious and justified, and how much is foreign or a product of imagination.

It will also be useful to look for the significance of the order of the runes and their placement in the Aetts. The deeper modern interpretations gain much from looking at the 3 x 8 arrangement.

6.2   Techniques

Not much is known of the details of the practices associated with the Runes, but there are general references to divination, magic, and healing in the literature.

Divination

Tacitus describes the practice of the head of the family or a priest who would spread out a white cloth on the ground, then throw pieces of wood marked with different signs. They would pray and look upward as they picked three pieces from the cloth at random, one at a time. These were interpreted according to their signs.

Tacitus is clear that the method is always the same. He was writing in the year 98 CE. The signs were likely to have been runes, as the oldest surviving inscriptions date from not too long after that time and show a well-developed system.

Most Asatruar do not follow the New-Age practice of interpreting runes that fall upside down as reversed in meaning. Many runes are the same either way up anyway.

Magic

There are a few inscriptions that seem to have a magical purpose. The Bjorketorp and Stentoften stones are the clearest, threatening any who disturb the stones with "deep" and "hidden" runes.

There is also the method of "bind-runes", which are formed by combining two or more runes on one "stave" or vertical line. This could combine the intent of the various runes into one spell. Although historical examples seem to be merely to save space.

Incantation is another method, mentioned in the sources as "galdr". We have no record of an actual runic galdr, unless some of the undecipherable formulae were meant to be chanted, but we do have many examples of old incantations. These were usually repetitive phrases in verse form.

The Old Norse word "vitki" is now commonly used to denote a rune magician. The word literally means "one who knows", or "wise one". It is related to words like English "wit" (to have ones wits, to be aware), also German "wissen" = "to know". A vitki could really be anyone with specialist knowledge, so "rune vitki" might be a more fitting term for one specialising in the runes.

Healing

There is mention of runes used for healing in the sagas. This is not surprising, as most magical systems have offensive, defensive, and healing uses. The cases mentioned refer to charms or formulae carved on an item to be kept on or near the patient.

Summary

Although the details of the old techniques are largely lost, the surviving descriptions indicate that they would not have been too alien for anyone who has looked at common forms of traditional or tribal magic.

This book is intended only to give the briefest outline of the possible areas of investigation. Each of the subjects mentioned can be explored further in books and web sites listed in the resources section.

7   Resources

Here is a selection of various resources recommended as a start for further study. Much of the material for this book has been distilled from these sources.

Included here:

• The three Rune Poems and the Runatal, original text & new translation with notes.

• Gothic Alphabet.

• Useful Web Sites.

• Books for further study.

• Popular authors discussed

The Anglo-Saxon Rune Poem
First 24 Runes

Old English:

ᚠ (**feoh**) byþ frofur fira gehwylcum;
sceal ðeah manna gehwylc miclun hyt dælan,
gif he wile for Drihtne domes hleotan.

Modernised script:

(feoh) byþ frófur fíra gehwylcum;
sceal ðéah manna gehwylc miclun hyt dælan,
gif hé wile for Drihtne dómes hléotan.

Modern English Translation:

Money[1] is a comfort to humans all;
but each one should deal it out abundantly,
if he wants before the Lord[2] to chance judgement.

---

[1] Wealth. From a word originally meaning cattle. Cognate with "fee".
[2] Drihten. Lord. Usually a king or deity.

ᚢ (úr) byþ anmód and oferhyrned,
felafrécne déor -feohteþ mid hornum-
mære mórstapa; þæt is módig wuht!

Aurochs[3] is single-minded and over-horned,
a very dangerous animal - fights with horns -
a notorious moor-treader; that is an intrepid being!

ᚦ (þorn) byþ ðearle scearp, ðegna gehwylcum
anfengys yfyl, ungemetun réþe
manna gehwylcun ðe him mid resteð.

Thorn is extremely sharp, for any warrior
to grab it, evil; excessively fierce
to any man who amongst them rests.

---

[3] Wild ox. Now extinct.

ᚩ (**ós**) byþ ordfruma ælcre spræce,
wísdómes wraþu and witena frófur
and eorla gehwám éadnys and tóhiht.

Deity/Mouth[4] is the origin of every language,
Wisdom's support and counsellors' consolation
and to any warrior gladness and confidence.

ᚱ (**rád**) byþ on recyde rinca gehwylcum
séfte, and swíþhwæt ðám ðe sitteþ onufan
méare mægenheardum ofer mílpaþas.

Riding is, in the hall, for any warrior
soft, but so strenuous for those who sit high upon
a strong hard horse over miles of trails.

---

[4] **Os** in OE is a **god** (as in ON "As"). In Latin, **os** is **mouth**.
The ambiguity is probably intentional.

ᚳ (**cén**) byþ cwicera gehwám cúþ on fyre,
blác and beortlíc; byrneþ oftust
ðær hí aþelingas inne restaþ.

Lamp is to the living all, known by its flame,
pale and bright; it burns most often
where the noble folk within relax.

ᚷ (**gyfu**) gumena byþ gleng and herenys
wraþu and wyrþscype; and wræcna gehwám
ár and ætwist, ðe byþ óþra léas.

Gift for men is adornment and complement,
support and dignity; and for all the dispossessed,
forgiveness and sustenance, who would otherwise have
nothing.

ᚹ (**wyn**)ne brúceþ ðe can wéana lyt,
sáres and sorge, and him sylfa hæfþ
blæd and blysse and éac byrga geniht.

Joy is had by one who knows few troubles,
sores or sorrow, and has for himself
reputation and happiness, and also a fine secure home.

ᚻ (**hægl**) byþ hwítust corna;
hwyrft hit of heofones lyfte, wealcaþ hit windes scúra;
weorþeþ hit tó wætere syððan.

Hail is the whitest of seeds;
it spins out of heaven's air, rolling with the wind's blows;
it is turned into water thereafter.

† (**nyd**) byþ nearu on bréostan;
weorþeþ hí ðéah oft niþa bearnum
tó helpe and tó hæle gehwæþre, gif hí his hlystaþ æror.

Need is tight in the breast;
but it often happens for humans' children
to help and to save each, if they listen to it early.

| (**ís**) byþ oferceald, ungemetum slidor;
glisnaþ glæshlúttur gimmum gelícust;
flór forste geworuht, fæger ansyne.

Ice is over-cold, extremely slippery;
it glistens glass-clear, most like gems;
it is a floor wrought by frost, fair to look upon.

ᛄ (**gér**) byþ gumena hiht, ðonne God læteþ,
hálig heofones cyning, hrúsan syllan
beorhte bléda beornum and ðearfum.

Year/Harvest is men's hope, when God,
holy heaven's king, lets the earth give
shining fruit to the warriors and the poor.

ᛇ (**éoh**) byþ útan unsméþe tréow,
heard hrúsan fæst, hyrde fyres,
wyrtrumun underwreþyd, wynan on éþle.

Yew is on the outside an unsmooth tree,
hard in the earth holding fast, fire's keeper,
by roots buttressed, a joy on the estate.

ᚹ (peorð) byþ symble plega and hlehter
wlancum ....., ðár wigan sittaþ
on béorsele blíþe ætsomne.

Peorth[5] is ever play and laughter
to the proud (missing), where warriors sit
in the beer-hall merrily together.

ᛉ (**eolhx**)secg eard hæfþ oftust on fenne,
wexeð on wature; wundaþ grimme,
blóde bréneð beorne gehwylcne
ðe him ænigne onfeng gedéð.

Elk-sedge is native most often in the fen,
it grows in water; it wounds grimly,
burning with blood any warrior
who, in any way, grabs at it.

---

[5] Meaning unknown. Could be a game or a tune.

ᚻ (**sigel**) sémannum symble biþ on hihte,
ðonne hí hine feriaþ ofer fisces beþ,
oþ hí brimhengest bringeþ tó lande.

Sun/sail[6] for seamen is ever cause for hope,
when they ferry it over the fishes' bath,
until the sea-stallion brings them to land.

ᛏ (**Tír**) biþ tácna sum; healdeð trywa wel
wiþ æþelingas; á biþ on færylde
ofer nihta genipu; næfre swíceþ.

Tir is a particular token[7]; it holds trust well
with noble folk; it is ever on a journey[8]
over nights' mists; it never deceives.

---

[6] Another intentional ambiguity.
[7] Tacna sum. (token some) = "A certain sign".
[8] Faerylde = Faring, a voyage.

ᛒ (**beorc**) byþ bléda léas; bereþ efne swá ðéah
tánas bútan túdder; biþ on telgum wlitig,
héah on helme, hrysted fægere;
geloden léafum, lyfte getenge.

Birch is lacking fruit; it bears even so
sprouts without seed; its boughs beautiful,
high on top, fairly decorated;
grown with leaves, close to the sky.

ᛖ (**eh**) byþ for eorlum æþelinga wyn,
hors hófum wlanc, ðær him hæle_as ymb,
welege on wicgum, wrixlaþ spræce;
and biþ unstyllum æfre frófur.

Horse is, before warriors, the joy of noble folk,
a horse hoof-proud, when the warriors around it,
wealthy on steeds, exchange speech;
and it is, to the wanderer, ever a benefit.

ᛗ (**man**) byþ on myrgþe his mágan léof;
sceal þéah ánra gehwylc óðrum swícan,
for ðám Dryhten wyle dóme síne
þæt earme flæsc eorþan betæcan.

Man is, in his mirth, to his kinfolk dear;
yet shall each disappoint the other,
accordingly the Lord wills, by his law,
that the poor flesh be entrusted to the earth.

ᛚ (**lagu**) byþ léodum langsum geþúht,
gif hí sculun néþan on nacan tealtum,
and hí sæyþa swyþe brégaþ,
and se brimhengest brídles ne gymeð.

Sea is by folk thought wide indeed,
if they should dare to go in a ship unsteady,
and the waves terribly frighten them,
and the sea-stallion heed not its bridle.

ᚾ (**Ing**) wæs ærest mid Éast-Denum
gesewen secgun, oþ hé siððan ést
ofer wæg gewát; wæn æfter ran;
ðus heardingas ðone hæle nemdun.

Ing was first with the East-Danes
seen they say, until he later east
over the sea departed; wagon followed after;
thus warriors named that hero.

ᛟ (**éþel**) byþ oferléof æghwylcum men,
gif he mót ðær rihtes and gerysena on
brúcan on bolde bléadum oftast.

Homestead is over-dear to each man,
if he may there justice and courtesies
enjoy in a mansion in frequent prosperity.

ᛞ (dæg) byþ Drihtnes sond, déore mannum,
mære Metodes léoht, myrgþ and tóhiht
éadgum and earmum, eallum bríce.

Day is the Lord's herald, dear to men,
the great Judge's light, merriment and hope
to the fortunate and the poor, enjoyed by all.

Although some of the extra Anglo-Saxon Runes have poems,
these are rarely used in modern esoteric practice. Those
wishing to know more about them should read "Rune
Games", mentioned in the booklist.

The extra verses are for:

Ac   Oak
Aesc   Ash
Yr   Yew Bow
Iar   Beaver
Ear   Dust

The Old Icelandic Rune Poem

ᚠ (**fé**) er frænda róg/ ok flæðar viti/ ok grafseiðs gata.

Money[9] is kinsmens' quarrel/ and flood-tide's token[10]/ and necromancy's[11] road.

aurum[12]
gold

fylkir[13]

ᚢ (**úr**) er skýja grátr/ ok skára þverir/ ok hirðis hatr.

drizzle is the clouds' tears/ and the harvest's ruin/ and the herder's hate.

umbre
shadow

vísi

---

[9] Money or cattle, indicators of of wealth.
[10] Kenning for booty. The flood (high) tide was best for raiding up rivers from the sea.
[11] Graf-seidh = "grave-magic".
[12] Latin word relating to each rune's meaning.
[13] Each verse includes a term for King or leader demonstrating the rune sound.

ᚦ (þurs) er kvenna kvöl/ ok kletta búi/ ok varðrúnar verr.

giant is womens' illness/ and a cliff-dweller/ and Vardhrun's husband.

    Saturnus   þengill
    Saturn

ᚬ (áss) er aldingautr/ ok Ásgarðs jöfurr/ ok Valhallar vísi.

god (Ódhinn) is progenitor/ and Ásgardh's chief/ and Valhall's leader.

    Jupiter   oddviti
    Jupiter

ᚱ **(reið)** er sitjandi sæla/ ok snúðig ferð/ ok jórs erfiði.

riding is sitting joyful/ and a speedy trip/ and the horse's toil.

> iter   ræsir
> *journey*

ᚲ **(kaun)** er barna böl/ ok bardaga för/ ok holdfúa hús.

sore is childrens' illness/ and a battle journey/ and putrescence's house.

> flagella   konungr
> *whip*

✳ (**hagall**) er kaldakorn/ ok krapadrífa/ ok snáka sótt.

hail is cold seed/ and a sleet shower/ and snake's illness[14].

    grando   hildingr
    hail

↑ (**nauð**) er þýjar þrá/ ok þungr kostr/ ok vássamlig verk.

need is a bondswoman's yearning/ and a difficult circumstance/ and drudging work.

    opera   niflungr
    work

---

[14] "snake-illness', kenning for "cold weather".

| (**íss**) er árbörkr/ ok unnar þak/ ok feigra manna fár.

ice is a river's bark/ and a wave's thatch/ and doomed men's downfall.

glacies   jöfurr
ice

† (**ár**) er gumna góði/ ok gott sumar/ ok algróinn akr.

year/harvest is men's bounty/ and a good summer/ and a full-grown field.

annus   allvaldr
year

ᚼ (**sól**) er skýja skjöldr / ok skínandi röðull / ok ísa aldrtregi.

sun is the clouds' shield / and a shining ray / and ice's old enemy.

       rota   siklingr
       wheel

ᛏ (**Tyr**) er einhendr áss / ok úlfs leifar / ok hofa hilmir.

Tyr is a one-handed god / and wolf's leftovers[15] / and the temple's chief.

       Mars   tiggi
       Mars

---

[15] How Tyr lost his hand to the Fenris Wolf.

ᛒ (**bjarkan**) er laufgat lim/ ok lítit tré/ ok ungamligr viðr.

birch is a leaf covered limb/ and a slender tree/ and a spritely wood.

abies	buðlungr
fir tree	

ᛘ (**maðr**) er manns gaman/ ok moldar auki/ ok skipa skreytir.

man is man's pleasure/ and mould's[16] increase/ and a ship's embellisher.

homo	mildingr
man	

---

[16] Mould in its meaning of soil/earth, as in the grave.

ᛚ (**lögr**) er vellanda vatn/ ok víðr ketill/ ok glömmungr grund.

sea is a welling water/ and a wide kettle/ and a fish's field.

lacus   lofðungr
lake

ᛦ (**yr**) er bendr bogi/ ok brotgjarnt járn/ ok fífu Farbauti.

yew is a bent bow/ and fragile iron/ and arrow's Farbauti[17].

arcus   ynglingr
bow

---

[17] Farbauti the giant, Loki's father. A reference to the way the bow flings the arrow.

The Old Norwegian Rune Poem

ᚠ (**fé**) veldr frænda rógi; fœðisk úlfr í skógi.

    Money[18] causes kinsmen's quarrel; the wolf is reared in the forest.

ᚢ (**úr**) es[19] af illu járni; opt hleypr hreinn á hjarni.

    slag is from bad iron; oft lopes the reindeer over frozen snow.

ᚦ (**þurs**) veldr kvenna kvillu; kátr verðr fár af illu.

    giants cause women's sickness; few are made cheerful by adversity.

ᚬ (**óss**) es flestra ferða för; en skálpr er sverða.

    estuary is the way for most on journeys; and the scabbard is the sword's.

ᚱ (**reið**) kveða hrossum versta; Reginn sló sverðit bezta.

    riding they say is for horses worst; Reginn hammered out the best sword.

---

[18] Money or cattle as indicators of wealth.
[19] Early dialect uses 'es' instead of 'er', and 'vas' instead of 'var', as in more common later ON spelling.

ᚲ (**kaun**) es beygja barna; böl gørir mann fölvan.

    sore is the disfiguring of children; adversity renders a person pale.

ᚺ (**hagall**) es kaldastr korna; Kristr[20] skóp heim inn (heiminn) forna.

    hail is the coldest of seeds; Christ shaped the world (the heavens) in fore times.

ᚾ (**nauð**) gørir hneppa kosti; nøktan kelr í frosti.

    need renders little choice; the naked will freeze in the frost.

ᛁ (**ís**) köllum brú breiða; blindan þarf at leiða.

    ice is called a bridge broad; the blind need to be led.

ᛅ (**ár**) es gumna góði; getk at örr vas Fróði.

    year/harvest is men's bounty; I guess that generous was Fródhi[21].

ᛋ (**sól**) es landa ljómi; lútik helgum dómi.

    the **sun** is the land's light; I bow to holy judgement.

---

[20] Thorsson changes this to Hroptr, speculating that it may have been the original word. "Hroptr" is one of Ódhinn's nicknames. No evidence unfortunately.

[21] Name meaning "one of great knowledge". Commonly used by Christians for JC, but may have been used for Heathen deities earlier.

↑ (**Tyr**) es einhendr Ása; opt verðr smiðr at blása.

    Tyr is a one-handed god; oft will a smith be blowing.

ᛒ (**bjarkan**)'s laufgrœnstr líma; Loki bar flærðar tíma.

    birch is leaf-greenest of limbs; Loki bore treachery's fortune.

ᛘ (**maðr**) es moldar auki; mikil es greip á hauki.

    man is mould's increase; great is the grip of the hawk.

ᛚ (**lögr**)'s, es fellr ór fjalli, foss; en gull eru hnossir.

    water is, when falling out of a mountain, a cascade; and costly ornaments are of gold.

ᛦ (**yr**) es vetrgrœnstr viða; vant's, es brennr, at sviða.

    yew is the winter-greenest wood; and is found wanting, when it burns, to ignite.

Havamal
The section known as the Runatal
My translation

Verse 138.

Veit ek, at ek hekk vindga meiði á
Know I, that I hung upon the windswept tree

nætr allar níu,
nights all nine,

geiri undaðr ok gefinn Óðni,
spear-wounded and given to Óðinn,

sjalfr sjalfum mér,
myself unto myself,

á þeim meiði er manngi veit
on that tree which no man knows

hvers hann af rótum renn.
from whence its roots run.

139.

Við hleifi mik sældu né við hornigi,
With no loaf was I spared, nor with any horn,

nýsta ek niðr,
I peered beneath,

nam ek upp rúnar, œpandi nam,
I took up the runes, screaming took them,

fell ek aptr þaðan.
I fell back therefrom.

140.

Fimbulljóð níu nam ek af inum frægja syni
Nine awesome songs I took from the famous son

Bölþórs, Bestlu föður,
of Bölþórr, Bestla's father,

ok ek drykk of gat ins dyra mjaðar,
and I acquired a drink of the valuable mead,

ausinn Óðreri.
poured from Óðrerir.

141.

Þá nam ek frævask ok fróðr vera
Then I claimed fruitfulness and became wise

ok vaxa ok vel hafask,
and grew and prospered,

orð mér af orði orðs leitaði,
a word to me from a word brought further words,

verk mér af verki verks leitaði.
a work to me from a work brought further works.

Gothic Alphabet

Although the Goths originally used the Elder runes, Bishop Wulfila later developed a Gothic alphabet largely based on Greek. Despite the new letters and letter order, they kept most of the runic names for their letter equivalents. Unlike the Elder rune names, the Gothic letter names were recorded.

a	Ᵽ	AHSA
b	B	BAIRKAN
g	Γ	GIBA
d	ẟ	DAGS
e	Є	AIHVUS
q	U	QAIRTHRA
z	Z	IUJA
h	h	HAGL
þ	Ψ	THIUTH
i	ï	EIS
k	K	KUSMA
l	Λ	LAGUS
m	M	MANNA
n	N	NAUTHS
j	Ϭ	JER
u	Π	URUS
p	Π	PAIRTHRA
r	R	RAIDA
s	S	SAUIL
t	T	TEIWS

w	Y	WINJA
f	ᚠ	FAIHU
χ	X	IGGWS
x	☉	HWAIR
o	Ω	OTHAL

From this we can see another source of evidence supporting the reconstructed names for the Elder Futhark. This alphabet dates from the middle of the Fourth Century, several centuries before the names of the AS & Younger Futhark names were recorded. The consistency over the centuries indicates that the rune names were carefully preserved by the tradition.

Web Sites

In order to keep the ever-changing list of sites current, I will provide a link on the Rune-Net page. This will take you to our current page of many runic and Asatru links. It will also have information on other Rune-Net publications, and supplementary information for readers of this book.

http://www.mackaos.com.au/Rune-Net

Rune-Net members will also have access to our members study site.

Books

This list starts with the more academic and goes on to the more speculative, but all offer useful insights. Most of them are available on Amazon.com.

Runes. RI Page. University of California Press. 1987.

Runes, an Introduction. R Elliott. Manchester University Press. 1959.

The Poetic Edda. Tr C Larrington. Oxford University Press. 1996.

The Poetic Edda. Tr L Hollander. Texas University Press. 1994

Edda (Prose Edda). Sturluson. Tr A Faulkes. Everyman Press. 1995

The Germania. Tacitus. Penguin Classics.

Gods and Myths of Northern Europe. H Ellis Davidson. Penguin. 1964.

Runic Inscriptions in Great Britain. P Johnson. Wooden Books. 1999.

Egil's Saga. Transl. Palsson & Edwards. Penguin Classics.

The Saga of the Volsungs. Transl. J Byock. University of California Press. 1990.

The Lost Gods of England. B Branston. Thames & Hudson. 1957.

Gods of the North. B Branston. Thames & Hudson. 1955.

Futhark. E Thorsson. Weiser. 1984.

Runelore. E Thorsson. Weiser. 1987.

Rudiments of Runelore. S Pollington. Anglo-Saxon Books. 1995.

Pierced by the Light. R Svensson. Flying Witch. 1998

True Helm. S Plowright. Rune-Net Press. 2000.

Völuspá – Seiðr as Wyrd Consciousness. Y Desmond. BookSurge Publishing. 2006

Rune Games. M Osborne & S Longland. Routledge. 1982.

The Elements of the Runes. B King. Element. 1993.

Authors

Here is a brief discussion of the better-known authors of books on esoteric runology.

Edred Thorsson

Probably the most controversial of the popular authors, Thorsson has published several extensive books on Runes in magic, divination, and religion. He has also published more scholarly works under his real name Stephen Flowers. His academic standard is high, and he does have a PhD in Germanic studies.

As one might expect from such an author, the books have plenty of accurate historical detail. The two best known are his first, "Futhark" 1984, and "Runelore" 1986, both still in popular use by New-Age and Reconstructionist rune users alike.

Thorsson calls his esoteric system "Odian", as opposed to "Odinist". While Odinists revere or worship Odin, Odians try to emulate Odin's discovery of the runes as written in the Havamal. To achieve this, he employs the idea of "internalising" the runes through rune yoga. These methods were developed by early 20th century German Armanic occultists Marby, Kummer, and Spiesberger, and have been adapted by Thorsson to fit the Elder Futhark.

To properly understand Thorsson's philosophical direction, we need to look at his long involvement with the Temple of Set, in which he holds one of their most senior ranks. Although he has made an effort in recent years to distance himself and his Odian efforts from ToS associations, and Odians can be quite defensive about being linked to satanism, the essence of Odianism can only really be understood in the context of its neo-satanic roots.

The Temple of Set formed in 1975, by members of the Church of Satan who sought to find a more meaningful purpose than pure hedonism. Under the leadership of Michael Aquino, the ToS developed an alternative to mainstream religious thought. Established religions aim at omniscience, enlightenment, or union of the individual consciousness with the all. The neo-satanic philosophers took this to mean obliteration of the self/identity, or complete annihilation. It must be noted that most long time religious practitioners do not agree with this simplistic interpretation. Rather than aim for union with the universe, neo-satanic efforts are aimed at the separation of the self, the "isolate consciousness" and elevation of the ego.

The ToS was instrumental in coining terms for the neo-satanic view. One is "antinomianism", although the term was originally used by Martin Luther in the 16th century. The other is "Left Hand Path", also an old term given a new meaning, much to the confusion of many.

Antinomian literally means "opposed to the moral law". Luther used it to define the Christian heresy that can be summed up thus; if good deeds don't get you into Heaven, then evil deeds will not get you into Hell, so anything goes, as long as you have faith you will be alright. The word has since been used by various sects to describe other sects when quarrels break out. It has been little known or used outside of those circles since the late 19th century. Neo-satanic orders like ToS have revived the word, giving it the new meaning of "against the established order". They also point out that, while they espouse an amoral viewpoint, they still encourage ethical conduct.

The term "Left Hand Path" (LHP) has also been used by these groups in recent decades to describe their position in contrast to the established religions, which they describe as Right Hand Path (RHP). The confusion arises when, like Antinomian, LHP has had different meanings for various authors at different times.

Originally, the term was used by Hindu and Buddhist practitioners to describe Tantric or Short Path methods, as opposed to the years of study and meditation required by the RHP traditions. The two paths were considered complementary by adepts, and students generally ended up in the path that suited their individual natures. Their goals were however, the same, union with the All. Although the LHP methods are more extreme and risky, many are willing to take the risk. Students of LHP practices have occasionally ended up with severe and permanent psychological problems, and this has led some to moralise against the practices.

Another source of confusion is that in many cultures, the left is associated with the unclean, or evil. Hence the Latin word "sinister", which originally meant "left", has acquired its modern meaning. So for many of the less sophisticated, Right and Left are simply equated with good and evil.

Now that the neo-satanists have claimed the terms to define their philosophy of separation/isolation of the consciousness, the majority of people are left with little idea what "LHP" or "Antinomian" mean when used by any particular author. Thus, while Aleister Crowley would have been seen as very LHP by the original definition, he is firmly in the RHP according to the neo-satanists, as his stated aim was always union with the All.

The first element in Thorsson's Odianism is its (by the new definition) antinomian, LHP, neo-satanic foundation: the isolate consciousness. The second element is the influence of the philosophy of Postmodernism. Again, we have a term that means many things to many people. The basic features of Postmodernism, however, are the idea that history is a kind of story or myth that has no real truth. Secondly, that people from different cultures can never really understand each other. Thirdly, its tendency to promote relativism, the idea that reality is "socially constructed". According to many postmodernists, tribal myths and scientific theories are equally "true". Of course, if you accept this, you are really redefining what you mean by "true". In his own words:

> "History" itself gives us many problems. In reality history is a poetic fiction of sorts. All you have to do is look at fairly factual aspects of contemporary history: Did Lee Harvey Oswald kill John F. Kennedy? The Kennedy assassination is perhaps the most investigated, documented and analysed events in history. Yet certainty escapes us. What are the facts? What then is the "truth" about the assassination of Julius Caesar? What are the "facts" of the life of Jesus of Nazareth? Even the external facts elude us and if they are known for certain a significant question to ask remains: "So what?" What do the facts mean?
>
> For meaning we must go to myth. Myth is not something which is not true, it is something that (for better or worse) is eternally true."
>
> (Article: "A Short History of the Revival of the Troth", Edred Thorsson, undated)

The ability to define reality or truth according to convenience, or one's own interpretation of myth, has deep and disconcerting implications with regard to the potential for indoctrination. This is really the idea explored by George Orwell in his book "1984". It is also the usual method employed by founders of religious cults.

In 1979 Edred founded the Rune Gild, based on his idea that there was an ancient rune cult that he calls the Elder Gild (see the Erilaz myth in the next chapter). The Rune Gild maintains a fairly small following, fluctuating around a hundred members, mostly situated in North America, with a handful in the UK, Europe, and Australia.

The title Thorsson chose for himself in the Gild is "Yrmin Drighten", which he translates as "world leader" of the Gild. Some have pointed out that the term Drighten was usually used for kings or deities (see the first Anglo-Saxon Rune poem, Feoh), and Yrmin (usually Irmin, or Old English Eormen) means "all of the visible world" or "all encompassing", rendering a more accurate translation of his title as "Lord of the Universe". It is unlikely that this is an unintended oversight on his part, and can only make sense in the neo-satanic context of the ultimate exaltation of the ego that Setians call "self-deification".

The method of Odianism involves alternating between rational academic study, and irrational or inspired states. In this way they hope to avoid the excesses of subjectivity of the New-Agers on the one hand, and the restrictions of the purely respectable objective academic path on the other. In practice, although they do start with better access to historical information than most New-Agers, their claims of authenticity for their inspired results are no less subjective.

To facilitate his Odian vision, Thorsson set up the Woodharrow Institute based in a purpose built shed on his property in rural Texas. In his words:

"The Institute then has two main purposes in the world:

1) to act as a refuge for displaced scientific work in the fields of runology, Germanic studies, and general Indo-European studies; and 2) to act as a think tank for individuals interested in making use of the scientific work as a basis for inner development. The Woodharrow Institute is a weapon in the struggle against both modernism and occultizoid subjectivism."

(His recent interview with Michael Moynihan)

It does seem ironic that he often speaks disparagingly about mainstream academic runologists as "rationalists" and "positivists", yet describes his own work as "scientific". Thorsson is deeply suspicious of technology and modernity, even calling the Internet a "realm of thurses (ogres)". For this reason, he has at times issued directives that those who want to progress in his system should move to Texas to attend in person. His style of leadership is distant, even indifferent, yet extremely autocratic on issues of interest to himself.

I did get the opportunity to visit Edred twice in the late 1990s and spent some time with him as a senior member of the Gild. The visits definitely contributed to my growing unease with the Gild and its philosophy. I resigned in October 2000.

Freya Aswynn

Born in Holland in 1949, Freya describes a tough childhood with strict Catholic parents, ending in nine years of institutionalisation with behavioural problems. Emerging as a young adult with no high school education, she taught herself to read English and German, and developed an interest in the occult.

Starting with spiritualism, she soon went on to study Rosicrucianism, Astrology, Cabbala and Thelema. At the age of 30, she decided that she would need to go to England to take her interests further. There she met Alex Sanders Britain's most public exponent of Wicca, and was initiated into his system in 1980.

In the mid 1980s Freya discovered Northern mythology and the Germanic traditions and was soon keen to learn about the runes. This period led to her best-known book "The Leaves of Yggdrasil" in 1988. With its feminine emphasis, the book was immediately popular among Wiccans and New-agers. The runes and Asatru had always been presumed by them to be a bit of a boys club.

Many Asatruar have criticised the book as being too heavily influence by Wicca and her previous occult involvements, also of relying on the neo-pagan myth of a matriarchal golden age in the distant past. It is certainly a book that can be put into the "highly speculative" category. To be fair, unlike many other authors, she does at least indicate that she is attempting to use myth and imagination to fuse runes and Northern traditions with "modern" methods (Wicca and ceremonial magic).

Much of her work amounts to free association. A good example is the way she associates the rune, and the god, Ing to England. Not in any academic way, she admits, but in the same way that she relates Ostara to Austria. She sees it as a mystical connection. A more sceptical view is that the old Germanic words just happen to sound somewhat similar to the modern English names of the countries.

Her book contains some carefully worded hints of a "Folkish" or race based agenda, to quote:

> "to penetrate the deeper levels of rune knowledge, one has to be born into the Northern 'group-soul.' The ability to work with the runes is passed on through the psychic equivalent of genetic memory, the group-soul"

> "it is of vital importance for the future of one's folk, and in consideration of one's responsibility towards one's ancestors, that any man or woman most carefully considers the choice of a spouse, who will be the father or mother of their children"

> ("Leaves of Yggdrasil", Aswynn)

However the bulk of her supporters have been neo-pagans and Universalist Asatruar, who are very much opposed to any hint of racism. Not willing to alienate them, she has successfully distanced herself from the race issue in recent years.

I managed to visit Freya in 1993, as a fellow member of the Rune Gild at the time. She had a large old 3-storey house in Tufnell Park, London, and had rented out some of the rooms. She called it "the Enclave". I ended up renting one of the rooms for a few months while on a work contract.

With her strong Dutch accent and colourful cockney idiom, she was quite charming at times, yet could be deeply suspicious of the people around her. She saw herself as a spaekona or oracle. She is well read in Germanic Mythology, but admits that her main source of knowledge is her own inspiration, and her personal relationship with Odin.

Kveldulf Gundarson

Best known for his books "Teutonic Magic" and "Teutonic Religion". Teutonic Magic, now difficult to find, does have a large section on the runes. He also has an academic background in Germanic literature, and uses this along with various sources of speculative and comparative mythology, to weave a rich tapestry. His use of myth and imagination has much in common with Freya Aswynn, and they did indeed work closely together at one time.

His education and imagination open up grand vistas of the mythic landscape, but leave one wondering how much of it really relates to the runes. Certainly, immersion in Germanic myth and culture are an invaluable source of insight into the world of the original rune users. However, it does become apparent, reading Gundarson's chapters on the runes, that this is his own very personal and subjective journey through myth and imagination, with only the most tenuous links between the substance of the runes and the mythical themes he draws from.

During my 1993 stay in London, Kveldulf did come to visit Freya on a couple of occasions as he was studying for a while at Cambridge. I found him to be interesting and passionate about Germanic spirituality. A small, elflike, androgynous figure, he was generally quiet, polite, and happy to talk intensely about his areas of interest. But after a couple of ales at the Rune Gild public talks, he and Freya were well known for egging each other on with shouts of "Odin!" much to the bemusement of others in the pub.

Ralph Blum

Blum is the most successful rune author in terms of sales, yet also the most criticised. His book, "The Book of Runes" 1982, was immediately popular, and still sells in the New-Age book shops.

He graduated from Harvard in 1954 with a degree in Russian studies. In the same year, he volunteered to be a subject in a government experiment with LSD. He has commented in interviews that the experience had a profound effect on him. It does seem to have influenced his early books.

In 1970 he published "The Simultaneous Man". A sinister science fiction novel about a Government agency using chemical, surgical, and brainwashing techniques to transfer the memories of a murderer into the mind of a scientist.

In 1972 he published "Old Glory and the Real Time Freaks"; a fun children's novel born of the counter-culture of the time. It has references to his LSD experiences, and could be described as a patriotic journey into American freakdom and adolescence.

By 1974 he had turned his sights on the UFO craze with "Beyond Earth: Man's Contact With UFOs". It is a book for true believers, and still considered an important text by ufologists around the world.

Blum's interest in runes started in the late 1970s after buying a set of rune tiles in England. He read up a little on the subject, and supplemented his knowledge with readings from the I Ching. In 1982 he published "The Book of Runes", which sold with a set of ceramic divination tiles and a pouch.

The bulk of the criticism against Blum is related to his informal approach. Blum did not set out to reconstruct or recover an ancient system. He used his limited knowledge of the basics to construct his own system. In the process, he ignored the traditional "futhark" order of the runes, and added the "blank" rune. These innovations caused an outrage among the reconstructionists, who saw him as cashing in on, and even corrupting, their heritage. (See Blank Rune in the next chapter)

He has since published books on "healing runes", "relationship runes", "rune cards". They all seem rather too New-Agey and vague to the reconstructionists.

Michael Howard

One of the first to jump onto the rune craze of recent decades, perhaps even pre-empting it slightly, Howard published a small manual in 1978. This was quite inaccurate in many ways, partly through lack of research, and partly through lack of proof reading. However, it was probably the best available at that time.

In 1985, he published a more in-depth book "Wisdom of the Runes". This book has the benefit of better research, and the existence of other authors in the genre to draw from. The book seems to be a reasonable middle of the road. It is not scholarly, yet is just informed enough to avoid too much fantasy. It is a fairly light and informal discussion of mythology, although the relevance of some of it to the runes could be questioned. Two disappointing features are his use of the blank rune, and the presentation of the first 24 Anglo-Saxon runes as THE runes, as if they are the Elder, only, or complete rune row. He does not make his reasons clear for either choice.

Howard is a prolific writer of all kinds of occult material, both before and after his foray into runes. He is probably now best known for his 1989 "Occult Conspiracy".

Nigel Pennick

Born in southern England in 1946, his first career was in biological research. After 15 years publishing papers on algal taxonomy, he decided to become an author and illustrator. He has since successfully published over 40 books.

Here is an author who provides plenty of interesting meat to think about. He manages to dig up an abundance of fascinating facts, most of them historically verifiable. The quality of his work and the clarity of his writing, seem to hail from his early background in science. In many ways, Pennick's books are in a league of their own.

Pennick has broad interests in the cultural and spiritual traditions of Northern Europe. He has published books on Geomancy, Sacred Geometry, various aspects of Celtic culture, and personal magical development. He also designs Celtic art, and has been involved in Celtic exhibitions. He is a Wiccan priest, and has been a leading member of the Pagan Anti-Defamation League. His books reflect his deep commitment to Pagan ideals.

Throughout the 1990's Pennick published several books concerning runes. Like the other authors in this genre, there is as much speculation as fact. While the research behind the books is good, it is not always clear at what point he drifts from the facts and into his own musings. A good example is his book on Runic Astrology. A great blend of detective work and creativity. With perhaps 5% of material from runic sources and the rest from better known esoteric traditions. He constructs a very workable and consistent rune-inspired system, despite the fact that there is absolutely no mention of anything like it in the historical sources.

Like the other authors mentioned thus far, Pennick has created his own world of runic "tradition", inspired by excellent research and artfully constructed, but a world for which he alone can take credit.

Kenneth Meadows, Sirona Knight, and the New-Age crowd.

While all of the previous authors have contributed in a creative and educated way, the New-Age writers have tended to pick the highlights from Aswynn, Thorsson, etc, and rehash their ideas, presenting them as genuine historical fact. They tend to avoid any research into the original sources, and show a very limited knowledge of academic runology or history. They often weave both the facts and fantasies of better authors into their own New-Age fantasies, creating an unrecognisable mish-mash. When they do manage to present another author's idea in context, it is often without acknowledgement.

As brief examples: Meadows displays Thorsson's invention, the runic "tree of life" diagram. He does so without mention of Thorsson, and in a way that implies that the figure is part of an earlier runic tradition. He also presents Agrell's Uthark theory as a Swedish oral tradition, with no mention of Agrell.

If we look at Knight's so called "Encyclopedia" of runes, we can read it beside texts from Thorsson, Aswynn, and others, and see whole pages virtually copied and pasted with a few words changed around. Not only is it devoid of acknowledgements, it does not even contain a booklist to give readers an opportunity to find the original material.

There are many other authors in this group. Unfortunately, they usually dominate the shelves of occult bookshops. Most of these books are full of unfounded and unlikely claims about the "traditions" of the Vikings or the Rune Magicians.

8   Myth Busting

Introduction

When systems are adopted for esoteric purposes, they seem to attract their own urban legends. Often it is caused by people trying to understand those systems in terms of other more familiar systems. Often people are just keen to put forward theories that seem to make sense to them. These ideas are taken on board by others, and soon they are widely accepted without question as established historical fact or tradition.

There are also many examples of manufactured histories promoted by occult groups to give themselves an image of tradition, age, or authenticity. This is not a new phenomenon, the practice dates back at least to the Rosicrucians around the year 1600. Like the Golden Dawn in the late 1800s, and numerous other groups at various times, who "discover" documents that they claim to prove the age and authority of the tradition. These documents invariably fail to withstand closer scrutiny, but adherents of the groups hold to them as an article of faith.

More recently, the trend has been for self made gurus & experts to acquire impressive academic qualifications, and even more impressive occult titles, in order to be able to dismiss any who question their claims. This undermines the academic system somewhat, as the "guru" will enter their studies with preconceived notions, and organise their research to support them. Most of their equally qualified peers will dismiss them, but the debate will create doubt in the minds of the non-expert public, and loss of confidence in the academic process itself.

I was lucky enough to meet Professor Ralph Elliot of the Australian National University, one of the world's best-known academic authorities on runes. It was in the mid '90s after attending his recital of the Battle of Maldon in the original Anglo-Saxon language. I asked him about the ideas of the more academic esoteric authors. He was familiar with the work, but a chuckle and the words "lunatic fringe" made his opinion pretty clear. At the time, I was a little taken aback. But after meeting some of the authors, and since researching this book, I have a better appreciation of his perspective.

Some Fundamentalists in recent decades have also used the tactic of employing academia as a means to gain credibility for their ideas. There is a well-known Creationist, John Baumgardner, who went to the trouble of getting a PhD in Geology, only to use it to attack the common interpretation of the geological evidence. Mainstream geologists are able to see right through the half baked theories of "Creation Science", but a section of the public will see this as an opportunity to question the facts that have been uncovered by the patient research of thousands of scientists.

We could ignore the issue, and leave folk to believe what they want. Is there any harm in sitting back and seeing truth as relative? I think there is. If we accept the fantasy traditions without question, we demean the truth of our own heritage. We would also be falling into the trap of our own fundamentalism, putting religious dogma ahead of truth.

In the early 1980s I, and others, wrote articles questioning the Wiccan account of their own history. It is clear that the system was invented by Gerald Gardner in the 1940s, with the help of some other well known occultists of the time. It was plainly cobbled together from identifiable sources, including Western ceremonial magic, Malay magic, and Celtic legend. The main sources for their legendary history were Leland's "Aradia", Frazer's "Golden Bough", Graves' "White Goddess", and Murray's "Witch Cult in Western Europe". All of these have been shown to be highly speculative at best, and complete fabrication at worst. No modern historian would take any of them seriously as historical sources.

At the time, our scepticism was met with howls of outrage, and virtual charges of heresy from the faithful, who still called Wicca "the Old Religion". However, a decade later, there were few educated Wiccans who were making claims about having an unbroken tradition. They now generally accept that they have a new (c 1950) religion inspired by older myths and traditions.

Other Pagans, looking somewhat down their noses at the Neo-Pagan invention of tradition, resolved to use academic research to revive genuine Pre-Christian traditions. This was no easy task as the historical evidence was fragmentary. However, the Paleo-pagans or Heathens felt that at least they had a genuine foundation upon which to build.

At the other extreme, the New-Age fashion for complete freedom with regard to tradition, was introducing and mixing all manner of fantasy with influences from every culture. Anything goes. If it works for you, it is true.

Perhaps the most insidious assault on sanity in recent times has been the philosophy of "post-modernism", popular in the 1980s. Fortunately, it has largely fallen out of fashion after the bankruptcy of the philosophy was thoroughly exposed in the mid 1990s with the Sokal hoax and its aftermath. Most varieties of post-modernism depend upon the assumption that people of different cultures and languages are not capable of understanding each other. Some even claim that they actually inhabit different "realities", and describe reality as a social construction. This concept of "cultural relativism" has been used to justify "politically correct" ideas that basically amount to apartheid, separation to preserve cultural differences.

However, the path of relativism can never be more than a recipe for self-delusion. No two people have exactly the same culture or language. Cultures always contain subcultures. Each town has its own dialect. Each family has its own traditions and ways of seeing things. Each generation is different from the last. If we accept that we all inhabit our own little world, there seems little point in looking for any kind of truth. If we reject objectivity, we are merely left with our own delusions.

Ironically, post-modernist philosophy has been used to underpin some re-constructionist efforts. Unfortunately, they do not seem to realise that this relativism really puts them ultimately into the same anything-goes category as the fantasy New-Age traditions that they criticise. Rejecting objectivity, they can only appeal to the authority of their own questionable Gurus and experts.

Even when there are old sources to work with, we have to be cautious. Some writers will just assume that the old sources are always reliable. Many of the surviving sources of evidence were written decades or often centuries after the events. They were usually recorded by Christian monks, who had their own agendas when describing pre-Christian practices. The Roman writers also had cultural biases and political motives. The study of the way history is recorded, including the biases and motives of the writers, is called historiography.

All of these processes have influenced the popular literature on the Runes. Every book on esoteric runology today contains much that academic runologists and historians would call highly speculative, or completely modern invention.

I do not intend to judge the validity or effectiveness of any of the invented traditions. This section is merely intended to look at the modern inventions so that the student will be more aware and able to choose what to accept. We should not be forced to base our knowledge on fabrication. We are free to use what appeals to us, but we should not claim complete speculation to be historical truth. Neo-Pagans learned the hard way that such self-deception only served to undermine their credibility.

My own involvement with the Runes started in 1972 after reading Tolkien. I have studied them ever since. Around 1990 I was asked by Edred Thorsson to head the Rune Gild's South Pacific region, and did so for the next ten years. In 2000, for various reasons, the Southern Region went its own way, and became the independent Rune-Net. In my travels in America and Britain, I was fortunate enough to spend some time with a few of the well known authors of esoteric runology.

My formal studies have included Mathematics, Physics, Psychology, and Linguistics. I have worked as a Combat Engineer in the British Army, a social research project designer, and I now work for one of the world's largest computer corporations as a network engineer.

The Facts

The first thing to do is to identify the original sources. What do we really know about runes, and how do we know it? This was the subject of the previous part of this book, the "Rune Primer".

Original sources include runic inscriptions, the rune poems, and the rune names. There are also historical references to runes in early stories and recorded legends.

Between the facts and fiction lie the interpretations of scholars from Roman times to the present, who each tries to make sense of limited and remote information. Even the experts of recent times have had a wide range of positions on key points, although the field now seems to be settling down to a greater consensus.

The most extreme academic positions on the runes were characterised by Wolfgang Krause on one side, and RI Page on the other, during the 1970s. Krause tended to interpret most of the obscure and unexplained runic inscriptions as proof of magical intent. He also developed speculative theories to support this view. Page, on the other hand, could see no evidence of magical use at all. Most current scholars consider that there is some evidence of an esoteric side to the runes, but that Krause's theories are fanciful and not well supported by the evidence.

As you read and consider the points made in this book, you may find that you disagree with some. Just be honest with yourself about the reason. There are several compelling reasons that you may not agree. You may have found new tenth century source material that is not yet widely known. You may feel a need to believe the myths as a romantic aesthetic. You may have faith in a higher authority, despite the evidence.

I do not intend to present anything particularly sensational. All of the information can be found and verified fairly easily, and conclusions drawn for one's self. I will keep the discussion fairly informal, and provide search words and phrases at the ends of sections for the reader's further investigation.

The Myths

The current revival of interest in runes really started with the runaway success of Tolkien's "the Hobbit" and "Lord of the Rings" in the 1970's. Although the books had been around for a while, the youth appetite for myth, magic, and fantasy exploded with the influence of the counterculture and its taste for escapism.

In "the Hobbit", Tolkien used the Anglo-Saxon Futhorc, while in later works he invented a rune-like script for the dwarves, and made other styles of script for his different fantasy cultures.

Tolkien was a highly qualified academic in Germanic literature, and brought a genuine feel, as well as many elements, of the original Nordic epics into his works. It was natural for him to incorporate runes, although as in the original sagas, they only play a minor role. However, it was enough to ignite the curiosity and imagination of young readers around the world. It soon became quite common for students to send each other runic messages in class.

By 1980, the counterculture had largely transformed into the more esoteric and more commercial enterprise we know as the New-Age movement. Also known loosely as "Alternative" (or "Alternate" for those with an inadequate dictionary), the New-Age milieu was ripe for the runes as a system of magic and divination.

In the meanwhile, Reconstructionist Pagans of the Northern Traditions, known loosely as Asatru, had been working on runic research within their own circles. It was inevitable that a tide of popular esoteric rune books would flood the market throughout the 1980s.

Although this was the first worldwide runic phenomenon on this scale, it was not the first time esoteric runology had caused prominent interest. Some of the most notable previous examples were Johannes Bureus in the 1600s, Guido Von List around 1900, and the Third Reich of the 1930s. Each of these phases brought its own particular style and preconceptions, and each added its own myths to the body of runic lore.

Modern esoteric runology is a melting pot of many sources, most of them fairly recent invention. There is nothing wrong with creative speculation, and using the imagination to construct a satisfying esoteric system. However, claims that such systems are somehow traditional or authentic are misleading.

We will now examine some of the ideas found surrounding the runes today, and trace their origins.

Divination

The popular method of interpreting runes written on pebbles and drawn from a bag, or cast on the floor, may be relatively recent. Our common modern method is probably based on the 1st Century description from Tacitus in which wooden lots with marks are caste on the ground and interpreted. Tacitus gives no clues about what kind of signs were used. It is possible they were runes, but not certain.

There are no descriptions of divination using runes in this way before the 1970s. Although the runes had useful names, and it does seem very natural to use them for divination, there is no evidence that it was actually done before modern times.

On the balance of probabilities, we could say that it is very likely that runes did play some part in divination. They could be read in the patterns of dropped sticks, or the cracks of bones heated over the fire. Also, casting wooden lots was a common practice. However, it would be dishonest to claim that rune-casting tiles were definitely part of the original runic tradition.

The Blank Rune

Perhaps the most hotly debated argument between rune users today. Traditionalists fume at the idea of adding a 25th non-rune. New-Agers like it. Where did it come from?

In 1982 Ralph Blum published his "Book of Runes". The book became a runaway success, partly due to the nifty set of ceramic divination tiles and pouch that came with it.

Blum claims that this blank rune idea came from a hand made rune set he bought in England the 1970s. He kept them unused for a few years, until one day he found them and started playing with them.

Blum decided to ignore the traditional Futhark order and three Aetts division (3 rows of 8 runes), and re-organised the 25 tiles into a random grid. Seeing no significance in the pattern, he decided to read them from right to left, and it happened that the blank tile was in the bottom left corner, thus last. It also happened that Mannaz was in the top right, thus first. These positions convinced him that there must be a deep significance to his new order. He then proceeded to use the I Ching (a Chinese method of divination) to assist him in interpreting each rune.

Traditionalists reading his account were horrified. Criticism was further fuelled by the fact that the book was such a commercial success. For most people who use runes for divination, this was their first, and often only, book on runes.

There are no references to a blank rune in any of the extensive literature on runes before Blum's book, so we can be quite certain that the idea dates to the mid 1970s at the earliest. There is certainly no evidence of a blank rune in the runic inscriptions, rune poems, or other Nordic literature dating from the time when runes were still in common use.

Search terms: blank rune, Ralph Blum, I Ching

The Peace Symbol

It has been claimed occasionally in popular rune books that the Peace Symbol was derived from the Elhaz rune, for some reason inverted, and placed in a circle. The true history is well documented, and does not involve any runes.

The symbol was originally designed in 1958 specifically as the logo of the Campaign for Nuclear Disarmament (CND) in Britain. It later caught on in the USA and elsewhere, becoming known as the universal sign of anti-war protest.

The designer was Gerald Holtom, a professional designer and artist, and a graduate of the Royal College of Arts. He had been a conscientious objector who had worked on a farm in England during the Second World War. His own explanation is the most believable.

The shape inside the circle was a stick figure representation of the letters ND (for Nuclear Disarmament) in semaphore. The semaphore code was used by the Navy, and represented each letter of the alphabet by holding the arms out at different angles from the body. He also said that he was expressing despair, as he imagined himself as the figure standing with arms extended out and downward, palms forward in a hopeless shrug.

Semaphore positions for N and D.

There have been claims by right wing Christian groups that the symbol has an older and Satanic origin, but there is absolutely no evidence that it existed before 1958. There was certainly no runic influence in the design.

Search terms: peace symbol, Holtom, semaphore, nuclear disarmament

Dutch Hex signs

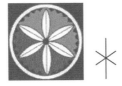

These have occasionally been claimed to have runic associations because a rather selective sample of them show a hexagonal symmetry. This seems to be enough to identify them with the Hagal rune of the Younger Futhark. If we look at a more representative sample, we can see that the majority of hex signs have symmetries other than hexagonal (bilateral, pentagonal, octagonal, etc). Also, even looking at the hexagonal designs alone, half of those have a horizontal axis, unlike the Hagal rune, which is vertical. Looking at some online exhibitions of the artwork, I counted fewer than one in ten had Hagal-like symmetry. This is about what you would expect from a chance selection of geometric designs. None had any other elements suggesting runic influences.

Typical Hex designs.

Before any further confusion, it should be noted that the "hex" in "hexagonal" is from the Greek meaning "six", whereas the Germanic "hex" refers to magic or witchcraft. The two words are not related.

The Pennsylvania Dutch, actually descendents of Swiss and German immigrants of the 1700s, did not start this style of folk art until the mid 1800s. It is quite likely that elements of their ancestral European folk art were incorporated. However, given that the immigrants were mainly from Southern and Central parts of Germany, who had not been in contact with a runic tradition for several centuries, it seems rather unlikely that there would be anything runic about their art.

Search terms: hex signs, Pennsylvania Dutch

Celtic Runes, Witch Runes, Runic Tarot

Here is a good example of New-Age creativity. Why shouldn't a word mean what I want it to mean?

For more than a thousand years, the word "runes" has been used to describe the form of writing used by Germanic people as defined earlier in this book, in short, the various Futharks. It could be argued that our runic ancestors would probably have called any system of writing "runes". However, today the word has a specific and useful meaning. It saves us from having to resort to redundancies like "Futhark Runes" to avoid confusion.

When we look more closely at these systems, we find that they fall short. The claimed "Celtic Runes" turn out either to be Celtic Ogham, Germanic Futhark, or something invented by the author. Runes were known in parts of Ireland after Vikings founded the trading town of Dublin, but this does not make them Celtic.

"Witch Runes" turn out to be a collection of pictographs (an eye, a Sun, a crescent Moon, etc). Each symbol may well be ancient, but has nothing to do with runes or any other script. They are a divination set, usually painted on pebbles. The system itself is most probably of recent origin.

"Runic Tarot" is typical New-Age mix and match. It would seem that any mixture of systems can be found in the "crystal dolphin" shops. Tarot decks come in any flavour, Native American, African, Tibetan, Wiccan, even Satanic. The runic decks are merely yet another flavour in the fairly recent fad of flavoured tarot. They are more likely to mislead than teach anything useful about the themes that they pilfer from.

"Runic Palmistry". Yes the book exists. Perhaps some may be able to see runes in the lines of the hand. However, put the word "runic" in front of any New-Age subject, and another profit stream emerges, as if by magic.

"Quantum Runes": New-Age/Postmodernist nonsense at its worst. Several books try to link runes and other systems to quantum physics. They invariably display a very basic knowledge of runes, and absolutely no understanding of physics. This genre is only for those who enjoy being baffled by someone else's confusion to the point that it seems like a profound revelation. Zen koans achieve the same effect with a great deal more honesty.

Runic Astrology

We do know that the Vikings used runic calendars reflecting the cycles of the Sun and Moon to keep track of the days of the year. We know that they could navigate by the stars. We even know that they had names for some of the stars or constellations, as shown by the legend of a star called "Orvandil's Toe". However, very little else was recorded about star lore, and there is no evidence of astrology as we know it, let alone any connection between runes and such a system.

Thorsson identifies the Rune Tir with the Pole Star. His translation of the Anglo-Saxon rune poem is fairly explicit. A quick search on the Internet indicates that this has become widely accepted as the definitive translation.

Tir is a star. It keeps faith well.
With athelings,. Always on it's course.
Over the mists of night. It never fails.

However, if we look at the original:

Tir bith tacna sum: healdeth trywa wel
with aethelingas,   a bith on faerylde
ofer nihta genipu,   naefre swiceth

First transliterating with the words' nearest modern relatives (cognates) to give a feel for the sense of the original:

Tir bith tacna sum: healdeth trywa wel

Tir be(it) token some(a certain one): holds troth/trust well

with aethelingas,   a bith on faerylde

with athelings(noble persons), (ever/always) be(it) on faring(journey)

ofer nihta genipu,   naefre swiceth

over nights' (darkness/mist/obscurity), never (betrays/deceives)

Now a reasonable translation:

Tir is a particular sign, that keeps faith well
with nobles. It is always on a journey,
over the darkness of nights. It never deceives.

It may well have been a star, planet, or constellation, but this is not stated. The pole star seems an unlikely choice as it appears to be unmoving in the sky, while the poem says Tir is "ever on a journey", implying constant motion. A more likely choice is Mars, as it was known to be the Roman equivalent of Tir as the god of war. There is no indication that the "sign/token" was necessarily used for navigation or astrology, although it could have been seen as a good omen, or friendly reminder.

Nigel Pennick has developed the most complete and impressive system of runic astrology. He includes a lot of useful facts from old sources, but the system is plainly his own creation. Others have borrowed from it, presenting it as "traditional".

Search terms: runic astrology, prim staves, runic calendars

The Wolf's Hook or Wolfsangle

This is an old German symbol often classified as runic. Indeed it does look like a bindrune or combination of Eihwaz and Nauthiz. It is even possible that the medieval designer had been influenced by seeing runes while travelling in Scandinavia. However, there is a more traditional explanation.

The symbol, sometimes seen in German heraldic designs, represents an angled steel hook with a cross brace, designed to hang in the fork of a tree at about 2 metres high with a lump of meat on it. If a wolf tried to jump up and take the meat, it would be caught on the hook. The cross piece is just to keep the hook facing outward.

The symbol dates back to the 1300s, centuries after the runes were used in Germany. It is fairly unlikely that it has any runic origins.

Search terms: wolfs hook, wolfsangle

The Broad Arrow

Known colloquially as the crowsfoot, this symbol is often found on British Army property. It is usually shown as an arrowhead pointing upward. I was tempted myself to look for a connection with Tiwaz, the rune named after the god of war. How appropriate it would have been. Alas, further research did not support this.

The mark, heraldically called a Pheon, represents the barbed head of an arrow or lance. It occurs in the Sidney/Sydney family coat-of-arms. It is usually depicted pointing downward.

Henry, Viscount Sydney, Earl of Romney, served as Master of Ordnance (1693-1702) under the rule of William and Mary. To help prevent theft, he stamped all government equipment with the broad arrow. He may have inverted the pheon to distinguish the mark from his personal one. The sign is still in use to indicate Crown property.

There is no indication that he knew anything about runes. There is no evidence that the Pheon or Broad Arrow was connected with the runes.

Search terms: pheon, Viscount Sydney, broad arrow

Origins of the Runes

One might say that there are two kinds of origin to consider. First there is the mythological origin, Odin hanging from the tree, and discovering the runes in a shaman-like trance. This has symbolic meaning, and reveals much about the Viking view of Odin and the runes. It must be remembered, before going further, that this account was written down by a Christian in Iceland a couple of centuries after the Iceland adopted Christianity, and a thousand years after the earliest runic inscriptions were made hundreds of kilometres away across the North sea.

However, most people are also interested in the historical origin. Although the evidence is obscured by time, there is enough to make an educated guess. There are obvious similarities between the rune rows and other alphabets close enough in time and location to have inspired or influenced the Germanic tribes.

The earliest inscriptions have been dated to around 200ce or a little earlier, but features of the phonology suggest that the system may have been adapted for earlier versions of the proto-Germanic language. It is possible that the runes were adopted as early as 200bce. At best we can say is that it was most probably a century or two before the time of the Roman Tacitus and his accounts of the Germanic people (97ce).

We need not resort to drug inspired gobbledegook about alien codes, or the runes existing outside of time, or being "ahistorical". The runes were developed from one of the existing alphabets that Germanic traders and raiders would have come into contact with.

A look at the Greek, Etruscan, and Latin alphabets of this period show many direct points of similarity, even identity. It is most likely that one of the many Germanic soldiers who served in the Roman army saw the usefulness of writing and adapted one of the alphabets he came into contact with for his own language. Just as Bishop Wulfila later adapted Greek letters for the Gothic language.

Search terms: alphabets, rune origins, etruscan

The Uthark Theory

In the late 1920s, Professor Sigurd Agrell (1881-1937) of Lund University in Sweden came up with a new theory. He proposed that there was a secret numerology of the elder rune row known only to a priesthood. The theory assumes that each rune has a number from 1 to 24 in futhark order, but that Uruz is counted as 1 and Fehu is moved to the number 24.

His evidence for this was that he thought it made more sense to start with Uruz as a symbol of potential wealth, and end with Fehu representing realised wealth. Also, he found inscriptions that added up to numbers that were multiples of seven.

It is not clear why this order should be better than starting with mobile wealth (Fehu), and ending with inherited/stabilised wealth (Othala). His interpretation of Uruz as potential wealth is not supported by any of the poems. Also, the number seven has never appeared to be important in the runic world, which seems to prize multiples of three and eight.

This theory was never taken seriously by other academics, and has not been widely used by esoteric runologists. It is one of those curiosities of the runic revival of the period. His books are only available in Swedish. Some popular books incorrectly present the Uthark system as an old Swedish tradition.

Agrell was also known for writing poetry in Esperanto (a failed attempt at an artificial international language).

Search terms: Sigurd Agrell, uthark

Galdr

This word is now commonly used to describe the intonation of rune sounds. It is an old Germanic word for magic, particularly spoken spells. The historical examples of galdr are usually rhyming charms, very much like the spells seen in fairy tales.

There are no examples in the old sources of magicians intoning the sounds of separate runes as described by rune yoga advocates. This idea first appears as part of the Armanen yoga system. (see the section on the Armanen next)

Search terms: galdr, galdra, rune mantra, rune chanting

Stadha

A term used by Thorsson to describe rune yoga exercises. There is no evidence of these practices before the Armanen. (see the section on the Armanen next)

Search terms: Stadha, rune yoga, Armanen, Thorsson

Armanen

During the romantic period at the end of the 1800s and early 1900s, there was a general occult revival that saw the rise of groups such as the Theosophical Society and the Golden Dawn. In Germany & Austria, the Pan-German romantic current was taking shape, inspired by the writings of Nietsche & the music of Wagner.

In 1908 Guido von List published "The Secret of the Runes". This was the start of the Armanen system. Like most of the occultism of the day, it contained many historical and linguistic fallacies. It was also heavily influenced by Theosophy and its Hindu Yoga roots. List claimed that the Armanen runes came to him during a stay in hospital in 1902 with bandaged eyes after a cataract operation.

The row itself is recognisable as a modified version of the younger futhark with two extra runes added. Rather than relying on the rune poems, List favoured the eighteen lays "ljodh" from the Havamal. They appear just after the "Runatals", where Odin finds the runes. List assumed that the lays must refer to the futhark, although there is no indication in the Havamal or other sources that this is the case.

Those who followed the Armanen system were heavily influenced by the occultism of the time. Many occult groups emulated the Theosophists in importing Eastern elements. Yoga in particular was all the rage. Yoga-like exercises were invented for each of the Armanen runes. These included body postures (asanas), chanting (mantras), and hand gestures (mudras).

There is an argument that a couple of rare pieces of ancient artwork seem to show humans in a posture that may be similar to the shape of a rune. Seen in a broader context, this "evidence" is very thin indeed. Even if the figures were intended to represent rune shapes, it is not evidence that such positions were actually adopted, or for what purpose.

Looking at the practices from the perspective of academic runologists, and experienced teachers of yoga I have talked with, the Rune Yoga systems are poor runology combined with even worse yoga.

Search Words: Armanen, Von List, Marby, Kummer, rune yoga

Metagenetics

Not to be confused with the health food company of the same name that had problems with the FDA. The term "Metagenetics" was coined by Steve McNallen in his 1985 article in a Northern Heathen journal (The Runestone).

It is unfortunate that McNallen is likely to be remembered for that particular article rather than his many other quite interesting and well-researched pieces. The theory of metagenetics is perhaps one of the most embarrassing pieces of muddleheaded pseudo-science to enter into the Nordic/Runic esoteric arena.

Although the original article did not involve runes directly, others have since woven the runes into the idea as a significant, even central, part of the ancestral "Folkish" psyche.

The essence of the theory is that each race has a genetic predisposition toward its ancestral religious beliefs and practices. He even posits DNA as a repository for a kind of race memory that he identifies with Jung's "collective unconscious". Indeed the theory is pretty much what Jung stated in some early works, that each race has its own collective unconscious, and that to adopt the mythos of another race is harmful to the psyche. McNallen merely adds the genetic pseudo-science to make it sound more up to date.

Despite his insistent protests that the idea does not constitute racism, it very clearly calls for racial purity, and logic would dictate the darker implications of this. As Europeans are not under threat from extermination, his concern about his people ceasing to exist can only mean their existence in a "pure" form. To quote McNallen:

> "We of Asatru are concerned about our ancestral heritage, and we consider our religion to be an expression of the whole of what we are, not something that we arbitrarily assume from

without. It also explains why those who do not understand us accuse us of extreme ethnocentrism or even racism- for it is clear from metagenetics that if we, as a people, cease to exist, then Asatru also dies forever. We are intimately tied up with the fate of our whole people, for Asatru is an expression of the soul of our race."

Also Thorsson:

"Runic (Mysterious) information is stored "in the blood" where it lies concealed and dormant until the right stimulus is applied from the outside which signals its activation. In this way, knowledge can seem to have been eradicated, but yet resurface again and again with no apparent, or apparently natural, connection between one manifestation and other subsequent remanifestations.

Scientists have more recently discovered the phenomenal platform for this noumenal process in the form of the double helix of the DNA molecule."

(From article: Secret of the Gothick God of Darkness)

Typical of New-Age/Postmodernist thinking, the idea is presented as having some kind of scientific validity, yet those who criticise it on scientific grounds are dismissed as "rationalists". I would not argue against a person's right to hold the idea of metagenetics as a religious belief, but I do object to the claim that it is any sort of science. Just like the creationists who put forward "creation science" to oppose evolution, metagenetics is nothing more than a rationalisation for an essentially irrational belief.

Even if we accept the mystical idea that runes are Jungian archetypal symbols, we are faced with the vague 19th Century notions of race, and the half understood ideas from genetics. McNallen assumes that we will object on the grounds that we see all people as the same. I would say the opposite is true; all people are different. There is more genetic variation within ethnic groups than there is between them. With each individual being so unique, it is not possible to neatly assign each one to the rather artificial and arbitrary construct of a particular "race". Human variation is continuous, without clear boundaries. Where is the dividing line between two neighbouring races, and what are the people who exist in between?

There is nothing politically correct about this objection, it really boils down to numbers. Although all of my known ancestors were fair blue eyed northern Europeans, each generation further back I find double the number of ancestors (2 parents, 4 grandparents, 8 great-grandparents, etc). You do not have to go too far back before the number of ancestors is so huge that some are certain to have been from different regions of the world. What genetics does show us is that there has been gene flow between populations throughout history. We are all of mixed ancestry. No single gene is unique to a particular "race".

More recently, McNallen has backed away from the genetic argument preferring Sheldrake's speculative "morphic field" ideas. It does nothing to change the underlying racism, but at least it moves metagenetics a step further away from being mistaken for any kind of science.

It is fine to feel pride in our heritage, and even a sense of ownership of the runes, but we do not need to justify the kind of pseudo-science that was prevalent in Germany in the 1930s.

Laukaz

The rune Laguz has been associated with an alternative name "Laukaz" (Laukr) meaning Leek. There is in fact an early document that supports this, the 10th Century "Codex Leidensis". However, Page and many modern scholars point out the vast majority of sources from different times and places are in agreement that the name of the L rune always relates to water (Lagu, Logr, Laaz).

Krause posited that Laukaz was the original name that was changed to Laguz to hide its magical nature. Page called the Laukaz theory "Krause's Fancy". Leeks or garlick (Laukaz) are known to have been associated with healing and magic, and it is tempting to associate a rune with them.

It is possible that the rune had a common name Laguz and a nickname Laukaz. However, it is just as likely that the Christian monk who recorded the Laukaz name from a second hand source misheard, or that the source was not that reliable. There are no original sources that explain any connection between the rune and leeks.

While it is legitimate to use the speculative Laukaz association in modern practice, to pass it off as part of the runic "tradition" is somewhat dishonest.

Erilaz

Another of Krause's theories was that the word Erilaz, which appears in a small number of inscriptions, had a meaning of "Rune Magician". This was taken further by Thorsson, who postulated a cult or guild of rune magicians connected with a tribe called by the Romans "Heruli".

There are about a dozen early inscriptions of the form "I the Eril, wrote this" (-az being the masculine singular word ending). There is no indication in the inscriptions that gives a clue to the meaning of the word. However, there is fairly good linguistic evidence.

It is accepted by many scholars that there is a linguistic link between the name of the Germanic warriors listed by the Romans as "Heruli", the "Erilaz" from the runic inscriptions, and the Old Norse "Jarl", Old English "Eorl", and modern English "Earl". However, there is still much debate and disagreement among the experts, many do not accept that "Erilaz" from inscriptions has anything to do with the actual groups called "Heruli".

If we look at the linguistics, the only viable theory connects all of these words to warriors or armies. The reconstructed Germanic root is "*Harjaz", = "army". The root word survives remarkably little changed in modern English as "to **harry**", a term still used in the military to describe repeated surprise attacks designed to wear the enemy down, or test their strength. It also survives in German as **"Heer"** = "Army". It is also the root word of the warriors of Valhalla, the "Ein**her**jar", and of names such as "**Here**ward" (army-protector).

The Heruli were "the army people", "those who harry", or "the marauders". "Ek Erilaz" almost certainly meant "I the warrior". The word obviously had a lot of prestige, and this is not surprising in a culture that valued warriorship so highly. The word gained further in prestige until it came to mean "army leader" (Jarl/Earl). There is a clear linguistic theme in which the meaning of the root word remains consistent. It is highly unlikely that such a word would have diverted its meaning so radically that it ever suggested "rune magician" at any stage.

There is mention in the Rigsthula that a Jarl should be an educated person, who should know runes and also magic, among many other things. It can not be interpreted as saying that a Jarl was a rune magician, merely that an ideal Jarl should be broadly educated. Warriorship was still the Jarl's primary business. Virtually all other sources place Jarls squarely in their military and political occupations.

Nothing in the linguistic or historical evidence suggests "Erilaz" means "rune magician". In fact the bulk of evidence points against it. The most widely accepted meaning of "ek Erilaz" is "I the Earl", indicating a warrior of high standing or a commander who is stating his authority.

Search terms: ek erilaz, Wolfgang Krause, harjaz, harjan, harjilaz. See also Oxford Dictionary of Etymology for Erilaz as origin of Earl.

Further Linguistic Information

Proto Germanic reconstruction (dating before 100ce)

*Harjaz = "Army" (cognate with German **Heer** = Army)

*-il- = "person belonging to" (cognate with English **–ling**) Example: Earth**ling**

*Harjilaz = "Army Person" = Warrior

Note 1: Cognate words = words directly related in form, meaning, & history.

Note 2: that **j** is pronounced as a **y** as in English "yes" (or the J in German "Ja") Eg. Har-yaz. Har-yil-az.

Historical Instances

Roman: **Herul**i, Greek **Erul**oi (dating from around 250ce onwards)

Runic: **Eril**az (dating from around 200ce – 400ce)

Further Evolution in written texts:

Old Saxon	– **Erl**	– Man, Warrior
Old English	– **Eorl**	– Warrior Leader, Noble
Old Norse	– **Jarl**	– Warrior Leader, Noble
Modern English	– **Earl**	– Noble Rank

All of these refer to warriors or military leadership.

Most Likely Evolution of the word:

*Harjil-... Heril-... Eril-... Erl ... Eorl/Jarl ... Earl

Army Person - Warrior - Warrior Leader - Rank/Nobility

Erilaz/Herilaz, Heruli Phonology

When the Romans asked the raiders "what do you call yourselves?" they would have answered "the warriors", Heril**oz** (plural of Heril**az**). A common effect in the phonology of words with such endings is that the preceding vowel is conditioned by the vowel in the ending as it changes. This happens as the mouth unconsciously changes shape in anticipation of the next vowel. This would have caused lowering and rounding of the **i** as the ending changed from "**-az**" to "**-oz**" (singular to plural).

The conditioning of the unstressed **i** would have made it sound like a **u**, making Heriloz sound like Heruloz. Hence the Romanised "Heruli" rather than "Herili".

The initial **h** in *harjaz was never dropped (eg. Heer), most likely because there were other words that needed to be distinguished from it by the **h**. Dropping it would have caused it to sound like another existing word. However, with Herilaz, there were no competing words. In this situation an initial **h** often becomes optional.

Erilaz is often transcribed Erila**R**. The final **R** indicates a transitional period as the Germanic final **z** evolved into the Old Norse final **r**.

Heruli/Erulians

The Heruli are mentioned a few times by Roman writers from the third to the sixth centuries. They are described variously as a warlike Germanic tribe, mercenaries, pirates similar to Vikings, and light infantry like the Spartans (complete with homosexual practices). They were associated with numerous places of origin from Scandinavia to southern Ukraine. In some battles, different groups of Heruli appear on both sides. It was assumed by the Romans, and later historians to the present, that the Heruli were a wandering tribe, that settled on occasions to form kingdoms.

However, it is not clear that the Heruli were a tribal entity. It is quite possible that they were different groups, armies formed opportunistically, like the "felags" of Viking times, only larger. Such war bands were not uncommon, and could consist of warriors recruited from several Germanic tribes.

The name "Heruli" is the Roman version of what the groups called themselves, most probably Germanic Heriloz (*Harjiloz). It is most often translated as "belonging to the Marauders", or "people of the army". It is quite possible that it was a generic name that was used with pride by many such war bands, in the same way "Viking" was used centuries later. Once the name had gathered a fearsome reputation, it would have been tempting for any serious war band to use it. This would account for the confusing variation in the sources that mention their locations and cultural features.

The Heruli were last seen returning to Scandinavia in the sixth Century. According to Roman accounts, they returned to their ancestral home without any problems, and vanished from history. It seems strange that after 300 years of wandering, a whole army/tribe could wander into the territory of other warrior tribes, taking land and settling without a fight. After a couple of centuries away, they would have spoken a different dialect, and would have accumulated cultural differences that marked them as foreigners. Yet it is often remarked that it is strange that there is no evidence of such an invasion in Scandinavian history. However, if that force had been returning to their families after three years of raiding, the lack of upheaval would make sense.

Some of the few points of agreement in the sources are that Heruli were always fierce, lived for battle, and had a nomadic existence. Whether they were the scattered remnants of one tribe, or completely separate war bands, there is no indication that they were interested in runes or any kind of education.

The connection between the Heruli and "Erilaz" of the runic inscriptions is speculative. The connection between Heruli (Erulians) and runes is pure fantasy. As we have seen, the only real connection between Heruli, Erilaz, and Jarl, is linguistic, in that they all stem from a military root word. This does not imply that they were the same people, only that they were all warriors.

Search terms: Heruli, Harjilaz, Erulian, Jordanes, Procopius, Prokopios

Neolithic Symbols

There have been claims that the origins of the runes can be traced to Neolithic symbols carved in rocks in Northern Europe. The clear relationship with other alphabets in the region at the time runes first emerged makes it unlikely that there is any direct relationship with pictographs from thousands of years earlier. (See the section on rune origins)

Summary

In the end, it is up to the reader to decide how to approach their study of the runes. You should not be put off by the excess of pure invention surrounding the runes, nor daunted by the idea of looking things up for yourself. A little research can reap great rewards.

One thing we can gain from our rune using ancestors is their practical and pragmatic approach to life. They were not easily impressed with clever philosophies or convenient fantasies. They dealt with the World as it was, and would expect us to deal with the World as it is.

A common theme in many movements, both New-Age and reconstructionist, is the myth of a golden age, a utopia or idealised world that has never really existed. Many forget that the vast majority of our ancestors were struggling to survive in the face of disease, famine, and violence, without any of the comforts, security, and medical help that we take for granted.

It may be tempting to seek an escape from an imperfect World, but it is far more noble and rewarding to face the real World, appreciate what we have, and see the wonder that is right in front of us.

Notes

Notes

153

NOTES

NOTES